# UNBINDING
## *your*
## CHURCH

# Enthusiastic Endorsements for *Unbinding the Gospel* and the *Unbinding the Gospel Series*...

"...with clarity and sound theological grounding, we are invited into a grand adventure....could be a watershed book for mainline Protestantism."
**Alban Institute, Congregations** *magazine*

"...the 'don't ask, don't tell' evangelism program will not reverse the trend. Humor, whimsy and joy in the faith will serve us better. Reese's book is written to provoke, to tease and to charm us back into telling our story."
**The Christian Century**

"Martha Grace Reese gently but persistently lures the Mainline back to the ministry of evangelism that is the heart of the church. Based on careful research and extensive listening, the *Unbinding the Gospel Series* avoids gimmicks and the trap of the latest church growth fad. They invite pastors and members instead to a relationship with Christ that overflows the banks of our often cautious and reserved congregations. These books can convert even the most 'evangelism-cautious' Christians into eager disciples who love others enough to tell them why Jesus is the answer."
**John H. Thomas, General Minister and President, United Church of Christ**

"Martha Grace Reese loves the Church. Hope for the mainline church abounds in these pages. She carefully demythologizes evangelism and then reconstructs it through common sense practices."
**Jim Griffith, President, Griffith Coaching**

"*Unbinding the Gospel* teaches us how to relearn the practice of evangelism. It's published at a teachable moment. Don't just read this book—use it!"
**Wesley Granberg-Michaelson, General Secretary, Reformed Church in America**

"Don't miss this one!"
**Evangelism Connections**

"*The Unbinding the Gospel Series* is a great resource for congregations. It is inspirational, motivational, and a great model and companion for congregations as they seek to be faithful stewards of the Gospel."
**Belva Brown Jordan, Philips Theological Seminary (formerly Harvard Divinity School)**

"The statistics Reese gives sober me, and they motivate me too. And her stories of vibrant congregations give me hope.....when you turn the last page, you can't just let this be another book you read. You need to let Reese's message affect you, and your faith community, and through you, other people."
**Brian McLaren, Author of Everything Must Change**

"The *Unbinding the Gospel Series* knocks one out of the park! Reese equips mainline church leaders with prayerful and practical tools needed to change the church through the power of Christ's redeeming love."
**Becky Garrison, Senior Contributing Editor, Wittenburg Door, Author of Rising from the Ashes**

# The Unbinding the Gospel Series

*by Martha Grace Reese*

*In more than 12,000 congregations in 50 states, 49 denominations, 8 countries...*

*"Evangelism" is anything you do to help someone move closer to a relationship with God, or into Christian community*

## What's Your Church's Question? *WHY, or HOW?*

Evangelism books presume everyone wants to do evangelism, so they tell you **how** to do it. Six years of national, Lilly Endowment-funded research in nine denominations have demonstrated conclusively that most people would rather get a root canal than think about evangelism. You can tell people to "go be missional" until the cows come home. They just won't do it until they **want** to.

*If we answer the "*<u>WHY</u>* share my faith? question, we'll start wanting to know "*<u>HOW</u> *can God use me to help people move into faith?"* Our churches can't share their faith until they're loving, relational communities where people (1) pray, and (2) talk comfortably with each other about their own faith experiences. Once our churches make this shift, we'll want to know **HOW** to share our faith. The **Unbinding the Gospel Series** addresses both the **Why** and the **How.**

**Take a Quiz.** Decide where **your** church should start. Think about your congregation. Check all statements that apply:

- ❏ **You** do evangelism! I'm going to alphabetize the Sunday School closet.
- ❏ Evangelism's why I left my old church. I don't want to embarrass friends.
- ❏ Nobody's going to make **me** pass out tracts.
- ❏ Evangelism is theologically inappropriate. It's not our ethos.
- ❏ Whoa! God's doing exciting things in my life and through our church! How can I help my friends connect with this?

**WHY** churches check boxes 1-4. **HOW** churches check only box 5. So, are you a **WHY** church, or a **HOW** church? [Martha Grace Reese, author of the Series and director of the Mainline Evangelism Project and the Unbinding the Gospel Project (the Lilly studies), estimates that 90% of U.S. churches are **WHY** churches!]

**WHY** churches can become **HOW** churches if they start with **Unbinding the Gospel,** then do an all-church saturation study with **Unbinding Your Heart. HOW** churches can move into joyful faith sharing with **Unbinding Your Soul.**

## *"WHY"* Churches START with *GOSPEL/HEART*

**STEP ONE— Church Leaders' Study:** *Unbinding the GOSPEL (red ribbon).* Start with a "test" small group study with leaders who you think will like it best. Optimal group size: 8-10 members, pastor leads. (DON'T preach or write newsletter articles – you'll only create resistance! Remember: In people's heads, "Evangelism" = "Root Canal".) Pastor: read the introduction and chapters 1 & 4 of **Unbinding Your Church** and skim **Unbinding Your Soul** now. They will help you lead your **GOSPEL** studies effectively.

- *Study GOSPEL* in small groups over eight weekly sessions
- *Do the exercises* at the ends of the chapters
- *Pray* with 40-day prayer journal after discussing chapter 3

red
ribbon

If *Gospel* helps, keep going! Move on to more small-group studies of *GOSPEL* with your church leaders and teachers (20% of your worship attendance).

STEP TWO—All-Church Saturation Study: *Unbinding Your HEART (purple ribbon)* is a six-week version of *Unbinding the Gospel* with a different individual prayer journal. We see significant changes in churches that bring the "unbinding" experience to at least 85% of worship attendance. Each week, for 40 days, people will:

purple
ribbon

- *Pray* each day's scripture and prayer exercise & work with a prayer partner
- *Study* a chapter with their small group
- *Worship* — sermon, music & prayers centered on the week's chapter

SUPPORT FOR STEPS ONE & TWO— *Pastor's and Leaders' Guide: Unbinding Your CHURCH (green ribbon)*. *Unbinding Your Church* offers "best practices" for small group leaders, prayer teams, youth leaders, pastors. It provides comprehensive organizational aids, coordinated resources for children and youth, worship, full music plans in four styles & 7 sample sermons.

green ribbon

## *"HOW"* Churches Use *SOUL*

*Unbinding Your Soul: Your Experiment in Prayer & Community (yellow ribbon)* is for:

- *Small groups that have just finished the E-vent*
- *New churches*
- *New members' classes*
- *Vibrant, growing churches*
- *On-fire groups in typical churches*

*Soul* is where churches reach out! Many people who aren't connected with a church would love to try a no-obligation experience of substantial spiritual discussion, prayer and community. *Unbinding Your Soul* prepares church members to invite their friends into a 4-week small group experience with short study chapters, an individual prayer journal, prayer partner activities & group exercises. *Includes facilitators' and pastors' guides.*

yellow ribbon

---

*Thinking of using the Series?* Review all four books at the beginning. *Unbinding Your Soul* will help *WHY* churches see a trajectory toward becoming a *HOW* church. *SOUL* is laced with 70 stories and direct quotes from a huge range of churches that have worked with the *Series.* See *www.GraceNet.info* for more info & resources.

*For*

*Russ, Elizabeth & Sarah*

*First Christian Church, Miami, Texas*

*Lochlin & Catherine Anne*

*and for all you pastors*
*who are willing to put out into the deep water*
*and let down the nets, one more time*

# UNBINDING *your* CHURCH

## Steps & Sermons

*(Pastor's Guide to the Unbinding the Gospel Series)*

## Martha Grace Reese

WITH **Dawn Darwin Weaks**
AND **Catherine Riddle Caffey**

CHALICE
PRESS

ST. LOUIS, MISSOURI

Cover photograph: GettyImages
Photograph of author: David Bjerk
Cover and interior design: Elizabeth Wright

Visit Chalice Press on the World Wide Web at
www.chalicepress.com

10  9  8  7  6  5  4  3                              10   11   12   13   14   15

EPUB: 9780827238145     EPDF: 9780827238152

**Library of Congress Cataloging–in–Publication Data**

Reese, Martha Grace.
  Unbinding your church : steps & sermons / by Martha Grace Reese ; with Dawn Darwin Weaks and Catherine Riddle Caffey ; foreword by George G. Hunter III.
      p. cm. —(Pastor's guide to the Unbinding the Gospel Series)
  ISBN 978-0-8272-3806-0
  1. Mission of the church. 2. Evangelistic work. 3. Church work. 4. Pastoral theology. I. Weaks, Dawn Darwin. II. Caffey, Catherine Riddle. III. Title. IV. Series.

  BV601.8.R44 2008
  269—dc22

                                                                          2007037505

Printed in the United States of America

# Contents

→ Read these chapters before leading your first study of *Unbinding the Gospel*.

\* Chapter 11 contains three of the E-vent forms available for free computer download at www.GraceNet.info and a master list of the specially formatted material for your E-vent. Your password to gain access to this material is printed on page 82.

# Licensing Agreement

The ***Unbinding the Gospel Series*** WILL change the way you think and practice evangelism IF you follow the guidelines, steps, and timetable contained in the books. We strongly recommend that you purchase a copy of ***Unbinding Your Church*** for:

- each *pastor* in your congregation
- the *E-vent Coordinator*
- the *Prayer Team Coordinator*
- your *Small Groups Coordinator*

Each of these key participants must have all the tools contained in these books to plan and organize a smooth and effective all-church study.

Purchasers of ***Unbinding Your Church*** are licensed to make as many copies as they need of the introduction and specific chapters of this book for all team members, small group leaders, office staff and musicians for one E-vent in your specific congregation (see chart on p. 41). Copying the book in its entirety is a violation of this agreement.

As a purchaser of this book, you are licensed to download one free copy of seven complete sample sermons and a full set of organizational forms from ***www.GraceNet.info.*** You may use the sermons for your E-vent in any way you wish, including preaching them verbatim. We have made these materials available online so that we could format them in a larger size, add color-coding and keep the price of the book low and accessible to everyone! Your password to access these downloads is printed on page 82.

# Foreword

What a promising project! Martha Grace Reese's "trilogy" may be the most useful resources for awakening slumbering churches that have come along in a very long time. She publishes them at a critical time in the history of Protestant Christianity in North America. Ninety-nine percent of our mainline churches have little or no effective engagement with people in their communities who are not yet people of faith, hope and love. Unlike their forbears, our churches' main business is no longer "apostolic." We care for "our people" — oblivious to the fact that, due to the secularization of the West, our churches are now placed in the largest mission field in the Western hemisphere (and the third largest mission field on earth).

The ***Unbinding the Gospel Series*** includes three resources: *Unbinding the Gospel, Unbinding Your Heart* and *Unbinding Your Church.* Each has the "unbinding" metaphor in common. It is an accurate and powerful metaphor. Like Gulliver, who was once tied down by so many small strings he could not move, most mainline churches are so "tied down" by their traditions, customs, routines, assumptions, perceptions, anxieties, passivity, denial, scapegoating and (yes) rationalizations that they feel powerless to move. And, keep in mind these churches are in denominations and traditions that were, once upon a time, great contagious movements in this land!

It occurs to me that our need for unbinding extends even beyond Gospel, Heart, and Church. For instance, many conventional Christians have binders — or filters — over their eyes. They mistake the masks that people wear for their real faces, so they assume that people are more "okay" than they really are. They wager that pre-Christian people do not really need to experience forgiveness, justification, reconciliation or second birth; or to experience the grace, love, peace or kingdom of God; or to join the body of Christ; or join God's movement in the world; or to fulfill the will and purpose of God for their lives.

Most church members have bound "tongues" as well. They, tragically, assume that "witnessing" necessarily involves "preaching at" people. They do not want to do that! They do not even *want* to want to do that! Most church people love conversation, however. When they discover that faith-sharing best takes place through conversation, their tongues are often liberated.

Nevertheless, Reese's *Unbinding the Gospel Series* addresses eye and tongue bindings covertly, while addressing the bound heart and church overtly. These books are rooted in Martha Grace Reese's four years of Lilly Endowment-funded research into all kinds of effective evangelism, including a study of the one percent or so of mainline churches that actually reach unchurched people in significant numbers. The work seems to embrace the full range of mainline theology and to melt traditional dividing lines. She and her colleagues stand on the shoulders of the church's evangelical tradition to help churches today find their way forward. So traditional features such as worship, sermons, small groups, prayer, testimony and narrative play prominent roles in the *Unbinding the Gospel Series.* Readers will see, however, the imagination and innovation expressed in these classic forms. Some features within these books are new, with little or no precedent. *Unbinding Your Church,* for instance, has a chapter specifically for church musicians, *by* church musicians! I noticed that the project commends resources in Spanish as well as English. I am embarrassed that, in the most multilingual nation-state on earth, recognizing any other language than American English will be regarded as *avant-garde.* This reveals the extent to which our churches are pathologically out of touch with the changing mission field around them.

*Unbinding Your Church* prepares churches for a sustained "E-vent," an all-church small group study, to catalyze the church into outreach. I expect such E-vents to move at least 20,000 churches into their first invitational foray into the community in anyone's memory. To keep the momentum, they will need to "institutionalize" evangelism as a "regular" ongoing ministry of the People of God. Evangelism — like worship, Christian education, and regular giving — must be institutionalized expressions of our life together. Furthermore, the churches that get really serious will develop a strategic plan for their future mission and growth. They will become local movements through the strategic perspectives featured by the Church Growth movement at its best.

Most important, this whole series focuses on "Real Life Evangelism." Christianity is not only, or even mainly, a fire escape or a ticket to heaven. The faith is a redemptive approach to the whole of our lives — this side of death as well as beyond. I predict that churches whose leaders and people are tired of net membership decline, and tired of slow death by attrition, will take to the *Unbinding the Gospel Series* big time. Reese is right that our churches are stuck. By my calculations, at least 200,000 churches in the U.S.A. are stuck. Alas, churches cannot get "unstuck" without their full cooperation. This series *can* help them regain momentum.

George G. Hunter III
Distinguished Professor of Evangelization and Church Growth
School of World Mission and Evangelism
Asbury Theological Seminary

# Introduction

### How Can We Replicate Great Evangelism?

I wrote a book for pastors and church leaders to study together in the hope that many more of us can learn to deepen our faith and share it (*Unbinding the Gospel: Real Life Evangelism,* Chalice Press, 2007). I have worked with thousands of people who have read *Unbinding the Gospel* in the seven months since the publisher released it. We have made important discoveries:

We can help churches — *mainline* churches — begin to do authentic, effective evangelism. The book actually works! Amazing!

*Unbinding the Gospel* helps most when churches study it slowly in small groups, doing the exercises. Start with the congregational leaders. Our people need the intimacy of small groups. They also need time and practice to assimilate new ideas and to begin to change their prayer and faith sharing habits.

The congregations that make significant, systemic changes have adapted the book as an all-congregational study after their leaders were trained. They work hard to saturate their whole church with new ideas, new ways to pray, new ways to share their faith. The "everyone together" spiritual experience is crucial. We don't do church alone!

Think of it this way. A lot of churches are stuck on a treadmill because we *talk* about faith, but avoid the slippery slope of a visceral relationship with God. We talk about prayer, but we're not exactly beating a path to the foot of the throne to worship our Savior and to gaze upon his face.

So *why* would our churches feel a little *dry* to people?? Hmmm. Curious.

We're not going to fix these abstraction predicaments by *talking* about them. We must change our habits, not just our minds! Our people need to:

1. pray, and
2. practice talking about their faith experiences with
   a. each other and
   b. their friends.

We need to get real. It's going to take some time, some organization, some soul growth and some systemic change in our churches.

We're figuring out how to change habits. I have worked with many churches that have adapted *Unbinding the Gospel* (a 10-chapter book) to a six-week, all-congregational study. I now see that there is a broad-based need to take *Unbinding the Gospel* to the next level — an all-church, small group study version.

I have great hope, and now substantial data, that these aspects of church life are replicable. Typical people, normal pastors, are doing great evangelism. Other typical people, normal pastors, are *learning* how to do great evangelism. My hope lies in the fact that evangelism isn't rocket science. It's faith sharing. We can learn to *connect* more deeply with Christ. We can learn to *talk* about it.

Think of it this way. A lot of churches are stuck on a treadmill because we *talk* about faith, but avoid the slippery slope of a visceral relationship with God. We talk about prayer, but we're not exactly beating a path to the foot of the throne to worship our Savior and to gaze upon his face.

So *why* would our churches feel a little *dry* to people??

*What are the Questions?* I have heard loads of questions during the course of these conversations. They are "How?" questions. "How do we lead small groups?…prayer groups? How can we integrate *Unbinding the Gospel* into worship, besides just a sermon? What else can we do to pull together activities for the whole church?…for the kids and youth? How can we take this book and sink it deep into the congregation so stuff will change around here?"

*Here's the Answer:* At least, here's *one* answer! I'm giving you my best shot at answers to these questions I keep hearing from pastors and lay leaders. I've written two new books that go together with *Unbinding the Gospel* to help you do an all-congregational study. We're calling it the *Unbinding the Gospel Series*. It is testing *well!*

*Unbinding Your Heart: 40 Days of Prayer & Faith Sharing* is the six-week version of *Unbinding the Gospel,* _with_ 40 days of individual prayer exercises. (This book has a purple ribbon on the cover.)[2] *Unbinding Your Church: A Pastor's Guide* (this book, with its green ribbon) is a pastor's and leaders' guide to an all-church study, with small group and prayer group process suggestions, worship, youth and organization resources to do an all-church study, or as we call it, an "E-vent!"[3]

### Why Do an All-congregation Study, an E-vent@Your Church?

An all-church, small group study creates synergy and momentum within your church. Can you remember the most powerful faith moment in your life? When you ask them to describe the most powerful spiritual experience of their lives, many Christian leaders point to a church camp experience, decades ago. A lot of them say that nothing has matched it since for spiritual growth, theological integration, or fun. It's wonderful that they experienced camp in the first place, but that kind of intense experience of God and powerful community learning doesn't have to stop with the end of adolescence. God will give it to us *now*. An all-church study is a saturation experience that can rival church camp in its impact on people's lives.

One pastor told me, "I can't explain the power of the synergy that exploded in our church when everyone was doing the same prayer exercises together, when they were all reading the same chapter, when the sermon took it a step further on Sunday. People were stopping each other in the grocery store and talking about the prayer they had both done that morning. Doing the all-church study during the fall, invite friends to Christmas parties and Christmas Eve. Who knows where this could lead in your church? I would love to hear your story. If something great (or ghastly!) happens as a result of your E-vent, will you tell me? (Contact me through our Web site, *www.GraceNet.info.* Please put "E-vent Story" as the subject line, okay?) I really want to know!

### We've Discovered Some Extremes to Avoid!

Pastors, thank you for your ministries, for spending your lives serving God. It matters. I want to say one more thing that I've learned as I've worked with pastors who are using *Unbinding the Gospel* in their churches.

The pastors who do the best job of helping their churches begin to do substantial evangelism move up and down the hope/reality teeter-totter. If they sit, parked in the dust at either end of that teeter-totter, so do their churches! Hope without structure has the substance of cappuccino foam. Rigid structure without flexible faith can quench the power and spontaneity of the Spirit. The key to helping churches change is to stay hopeful and flexible, and to provide habit-changing structure. Keep that teeter-totter moving!

Some pastors do more than strike a shaky balance on the hope/reality teeter-totter. They pirouette on that board like Fred Astaire or Ginger Rogers (same steps, but backwards, in heels)! Most of us need a *couple* more dance lessons before we start dipping and twirling. This book is my attempt to help you move into the fluid, structured, acrobatic type of pastoring that promises the best chance to help your church change. That sounds cute, but abstract, doesn't it? All right. Sometimes it helps us to see what *doesn't* work in order to catch the vision of what might be helpful in our specific situations.

### How Could We Shoot Ourselves in the Foot?

Here are the two main reasons I see pastors sitting on the teeter-totter, smiling and nodding as they read their copies of *Unbinding the Gospel,* rear ends planted firmly in playground dust.

#### *Hope Pastors*

The "hope end" pastors have a tendency to grab *Unbinding the Gospel* off shelves. Boy! Do *they* move quickly! They read it on an airplane on Wednesday. They say "Wow! *Everyone* in my church could get these ideas! This is *great*!" They scribble out a newsletter

**E-vent Essentials**

1. Train leaders first *(Unbinding the Gospel,* 8–24 weeks)
2. Prepare for the E-vent slowly (16 weeks)
3. All studies — slow and experiential
4. Pray seriously
5. E-vent itself is a Sabbath (6 weeks)
6. Don't overload on activities!

The pastors who do the best job of helping their churches begin to do substantial evangelism move up and down the hope/reality teeter-totter. If they sit, parked in the dust at either end of that teeter-totter, so do their churches! Hope without structure has the substance of cappuccino foam. Rigid structure without flexible faith can quench the power and spontaneity of the Spirit. The key to helping churches change is to stay hopeful and flexible, and to provide habit-changing structure. Keep that teeter-totter moving!

article as they gulp their diet Cokes and gobble airline peanuts. They write sermons straight out of chapter 2 on Thursday. On Sunday, they tell their people to go do evangelism. Then they go do something else. But most of their people keep *not* doing evangelism. Huhhh. Curious.

I don't mean to be rude here to my "hope end of the teeter-totter" brothers and sisters. (Remember, I'm the one operating with the "Jane Austen *must* still be out there" magical thinking.) I *certainly* don't want to suggest that my book, your sermons and all those excited conversations aren't brilliant, fascinating, scintillating. But we may need to stroll down to the reality end of the teeter-totter for just a moment. I think we've uncovered one *slightly* unrealistic, unconscious expectation that may be sabotaging the effectiveness of a lot of our ministries.

Many of us work out of an unconscious expectation that if we tell someone something, if we hammer home a persuasive point in a sermon (or book), that the people we serve are going to rush out and start doing it. They *may* go right out the door and start doing it. But that's usually if we're telling them to go to the all-church luncheon that starts right after the second service.

If the sermon (or book) contains the word *"evangelism,"* odds are pretty good that all those people who gaze at us with such rapt attention may *not* race out and do it. Not any time soon.

It's going to take more than pastors reading **Unbinding the Gospel** one afternoon, thinking it's great, then mentioning it in a sermon. The very idea of evangelism, the "E word," "That Which Must Not Be Named in Mainline Churches," is too scary to most of our people. Most of our people need a conversion experience in relationship to the very *word "evangelism"* before they can hear anything we say about sharing our faith.

Josh Lyman was one of the characters on *The West Wing* (a TV show). Relationships with women were not his strong suit. Josh was a brilliant political strategist. He was also naive, avoidant, romantic, smitten, goofy (an extreme case of a "hope end" kind of guy). Donna Moss, his administrative assistant, finally laid it out for him, in a tone of utter frustration. "Look, Josh, you have to ask her out on a *date.* You can't just keep randomly tumbling into women *sideways,* then waiting for them to break *up* with you, like you *always* do."[4]

Let's think about the way we approach evangelism for a moment. Could we go about it intentionally?...slowly?...over time? Will we give strategic attention to training our people to have a spiritual life?...to learn to articulate their faith? Could we give them a viable opportunity to change their minds *and* their habits — all together, at the same time? Could we pray and plan so that instead of vaguely expecting total strangers to drop by our churches uninvited some day, we intentionally *ask* them to come, prepare the party for them, and make a place for them in our churches and in our lives?

What if we really *meant* it when we said we wanted to do evangelism? What if we actually asked people out on a date, instead of just waiting for them to randomly tumble into us sideways and hoping they break up with us soon, like we always do?

### Reality End Glitches?

Dearest reality end pastors —

How might you end up sitting on the ground at *your* end of the teeter-totter? From everything I've seen, you'll understand the need to structure your people's experience. You won't just talk to your people one day and expect them to change their habits by next Tuesday. You'll understand the need for classes and steps and structure. If *you* mess up, you're much more likely to have a blind spot that could make you miss the need for flexibility, fluidity, change, experimentation, trust, flowing with the Spirit!

Whatever you do, *don't* take this book too seriously! (Okay, take it seriously, but don't take it *literally*.)

The part of *Unbinding Your Church* that matters is the long, slow, step-by-step process. Be ready to ditch a lot of specifics! The sample sermons Dawn Weaks wrote are suggestions, from *one* pastor, from *one* preaching tradition. So are all the fabulous music plans that four different musicians have played out for you. The idea of doing an "E-vent," sermons, prayer walls, vigils, kids' activities and inviting friends to a celebration at the end are just ideas.

You may need to do something completely different.

The important thing is that

first leaders,

then the whole congregation

work on this book themselves,

in small groups,

over time,

doing the exercises!

Remember: the point of the E-vent is to help your members deepen their faith so that they have something to share. Then they can take the first steps toward sharing their faith, toward real evangelism that can change lives.

After that, you have to do what works for your church.

A while ago, a large church called me to discuss using ***Unbinding the Gospel*** for an all-church study. I invited them to be a "test" congregation. So I gave them all the materials for ***Unbinding Your Heart*** and ***Unbinding Your Church.*** They decided to do the study

Pastor's Guide with their leaders first
> then the whole congregation
>> in small groups
>>> over time
>>>> doing the exercises.

*Include these essentials, if you want to help your congregation change and actually start doing effective evangelism.* Churches that skim over these essentials may have a nice experience, but the experience doesn't tend to make much of a dent in their church's preexisting patterns. Why do all this work for nothing?

Perfect! See? It's the essentials!

University Church told me that they were going to do their study in the context of trying to discern where God is calling their congregation in their next major phase of ministry. They just finished a massive building project. The senior pastor of almost 20 years has announced that he is willing to stay with the church two to four more years before he retires. He'll stay ***if*** the church feels called to work on discernment for the future, and transition toward that change. He's too intense to coast!

Elizabeth, their associate pastor, called me several weeks later. She worried that doing an E-vent with the activities, sermons and worship designs in ***Unbinding Your Church*** might feel manipulative to people, that they might feel railroaded into designating "evangelism" as their call to the future.

She's exactly right. It could ***feel*** manipulative to people because at this moment in University Church's life, it would ***be*** manipulative! Their people need to be asking God what they should focus on next, not presuming that God is going to tell them that evangelism should be the most important expression of their next phase of ministry.

Studying ***Unbinding Your Heart*** in small groups and doing the 40 days of individual prayer exercises is perfect for them. The thoughts for pastors (chapters 1 & 2), the organizational ideas (chapter 3), the small group process ideas (chapter 4), the Prayer Team processes (chapter 5), the youth ideas (chapter 6) outlined in ***Unbinding Your Church*** should work beautifully. But University Church ought to construct their own sermons and congregational events that help focus attention on the book's prayer, discernment, community, and congregational systems themes.

***What would a discernment-focused E-vent look like?*** What if University Church emphasized the prayer wall and prayer vigil suggestions? Instead of a celebration at the end to which to invite friends, how about a one-day prayer retreat for the entire church? What if the leaders began with a leadership retreat Friday at dinner? The rest of the congregation could begin a 24-hour prayer vigil at the same time. The entire congregation could gather on Saturday morning to pray and discern together about where God is calling the church. They could ask the Spirit what specific steps they should take next. End the vigil and the retreat late Saturday afternoon.

The next morning in worship, the senior pastor could preach a great sermon, summarizing what God has taught the congregation, where Christ is leading them.

What would a sermon series trajectory look like for University Church's six-week, all-congregation study of *Unbinding Your Heart?* Here's one possibility. Each sermon would match the themes of that week's chapter:

> What if we opened ourselves to be vehicles for the Spirit? God can do miracles through us that we cannot imagine yet. We leaders can each say "yes" or "no" to God. Something real, powerful, creative, new, is beginning. We can each play a role in it.

- Introductory sermon for "Sign-up Sunday" (Six weeks before they start the study): We're going to discern God's call for our next phase of ministry together. Will you help? Will you pray together and join a small group? God has new ideas for us! Let's find out what God has in mind, together!
- Week 1: What is my faith? Who is Christ in my life? Why does being a Christian matter?
- Week 2: Prayer — we at University Church have seen what prayer can do! Where could God lead us next?
- Week 3: Real life in Christ — What can it look like here? What's most vibrant about us as a church? Where are we still a little fakey, a little plastic?
- Week 4: What do new members want? People in this community need Christ, they yearn to be accepted and loved. Do we care?
- Week 5: How are we doing as a church? What are our greatest strengths? What are our most profound weaknesses? What about us makes God say "Hurray!"? What would God change in us or in what we're doing?

*[Prayer Vigil and Congregation's Retreat]*

- Week 6: Okay, we had our retreat. We heard these words from God _____; we felt these nudges from the Spirit _____. Shall we go together? It won't all be easy. There will be wind, waves and currents to navigate, but if we're with Christ, it will be great! Are you ready? All right, let's go!

Do you see how University Church could have sat in the dust at the "detail/routine/statistics/this-is-the-**plan**" end of the teeter-totter? Elizabeth is a reality end pastor. And she prays, big time! She felt that something in the plan wasn't right for their congregation. She perceived that they needed to do something else. Her instincts were spectacular!

*Reality Pastors* — stay open to the Spirit. Be ready to scrap the plan and do something else!

*Hope Pastors* — slow down and focus! We must put structures in place. We need to routinize some of this creativity if we expect it to change people's lives. *Reality Pastors* — you don't need to do all this work yourselves. The Spirit will do much of the heavy lifting of evangelism. Keep listening. Pastors: we have two jobs. We must pray, love God, trust, hope against hope, believe in miracles and follow the leadings of the Spirit. *And* we must think, prepare, organize, communicate, educate, train and plan strategically.

### God's Doing Something Different

The Mainline Evangelism Project and our experience with *Unbinding the Gospel* showed that entire churches are ready to pray and to begin to talk about their faith with others. Mainline churches are ripe to slow down and pray. They're poised to get intentional about prayer and faith sharing.

I've visited many cities and spoken with thousands of church people during the last few years. I have a hard time even articulating this, because it feels new and fragile. But the Spirit is beginning to do things all over the country, in all sorts of churches — yes, mainline churches! I was concerned that I was making this up out of my own fevered imagination, so I have spoken with gifted church leaders with deep insight and broad exposure to the church. They see something new, too. Many of us are experiencing hope grounded in reality. God is at work.

How will we respond? In some ways, mainline churches have operated like a minority political party, the "loyal opposition" for too long. We have critiqued, held back and said what's wrong with *other* parts of Christ's church. Many of the things we've said may have a lot of truth in them. But it's the holding back that's the problem. That's us planted in playground dust. Many of us haven't done as good a job putting our beliefs and lives on the line to follow the Spirit. We don't have a lot of experience leading in new, positive directions. It is

How will we respond? In some ways, mainline churches have operated like a minority political party, the "loyal opposition" for too long. We have critiqued, held back and said what's wrong with *other* parts of Christ's church. Many of the things we've said may have a lot of truth in them. But it's the holding back that's the problem. That's us planted in playground dust.

going to take vast, divinely inspired imagination for us to shift if we want God to use us in powerful, creative ways for *new* things.

What if we opened ourselves to be vehicles for the Spirit? I don't want to sound any more grandiose than I can help, but I think God can do miracles through us that we cannot imagine yet. We leaders can each say "yes" or "no" to God. Something real, powerful, creative, new, is beginning. We can each play a role in it.

Will you pray? Will you let God show you new ways to lead and serve? Will you ask people from other parts of Christ's church to teach you things we don't know well, particularly about prayer and following Christ every step of the way? Could you help the people you serve begin to connect so deeply with Christ that they will let the Spirit use them, too?

Who knows where God is leading us? I know one thing. I want to be part of it.

Many of us haven't done as good a job putting our beliefs and lives on the line to follow the Spirit. We don't have a lot of experience leading in new, positive directions. It is going to take vast, divinely inspired imagination for us to shift if we want God to use us in powerful, creative ways for *new* things.

[1]I laughed out loud until the dogs stared at me when I read Nevada Barr's (mystery writer, national park ranger and recent convert to Christianity) recollection that her friend Debra defined optimism as "walking into a bookstore thinking, 'Hey, maybe there'll be a new Jane Austen.'" Nevada Barr, *Seeking Enlightenment…Hat by Hat* (New York: Berkley Books, 2003), 23.

[2]Martha Grace Reese, *Unbinding Your Heart: 40 Days of Prayer & Faith Sharing* (St. Louis: Chalice Press, 2008).

[3]Martha Grace Reese, *Unbinding Your Church: A Pastor's Guide* (St. Louis: Chalice Press, 2008).

[4]*The West Wing, Third Season,* Warner Brothers, 2004.

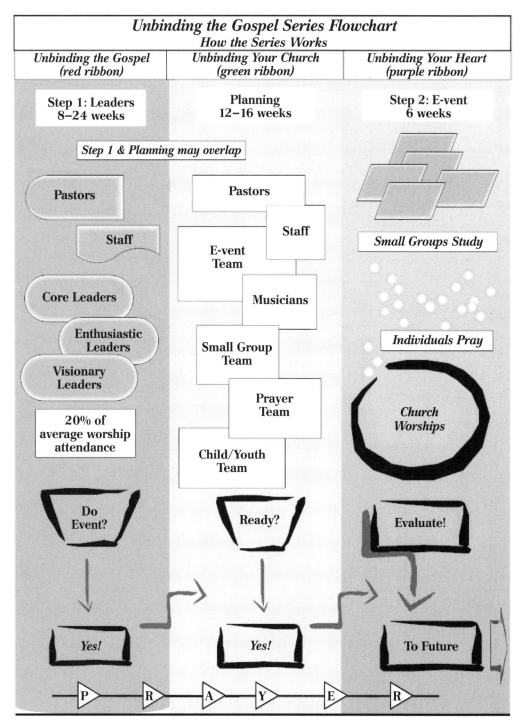

**Unbinding the Gospel Series Flowchart**
**How the Series Works**

| Unbinding the Gospel (red ribbon) | Unbinding Your Church (green ribbon) | Unbinding Your Heart (purple ribbon) |
|---|---|---|
| Step 1: Leaders 8–24 weeks | Planning 12–16 weeks | Step 2: E-vent 6 weeks |

*Step 1 & Planning may overlap*

Pastors

Staff

Core Leaders

Enthusiastic Leaders

Visionary Leaders

20% of average worship attendance

Do Event?

*Yes!*

Pastors

Staff

E-vent Team

Musicians

Small Group Team

Prayer Team

Child/Youth Team

Ready?

*Yes!*

*Small Groups Study*

*Individuals Pray*

*Church Worships*

Evaluate!

To Future

P R A Y E R

Pastor Form #2 from www.GraceNet.info, © 2007 by GraceNet, Inc.

(This and other E-vent forms available at www.GraceNet.info.)

# Unbinding Your Church

# PART ONE

## The E-vent@Your Church

### *Advice for Pastors and Leaders*

- **PART ONE** explores why and how to help your church start to do evangelism. How can you work effectively with your church to plan an all-congregation prayer and faith sharing study? What is the best timing, pacing, style of leadership for small groups? for prayer groups? for youth and children? How do you organize an E-vent?

- **PART TWO** provides examples of an integrated, all-church study. Reinforce individual, small group prayer and faith sharing with congregational worship. See sermons, scriptures, prayers and integrated music plans. Part II will also provide you with forms, lists and organizational aids to help you prepare for an integrated, effective E-vent.

*Jesus got into one of the boats, the one belonging to Simon, and asked him to put out a little way from the shore. Then he sat down and taught the crowds from the boat. When he had finished speaking, he said to Simon, "Put out into the deep water and let down your nets for a catch." Simon answered, "Master, we have worked all night long but have caught nothing. Yet if you say so, I will let down the nets."*

*Luke 5:3–5*

…one thing I do, forgetting what lies behind and straining forward to what lies ahead, I press on toward the goal for the prize of the upward call of God in Christ Jesus.

*Philippians 3:13b–14 (RSV)*

Unless the LORD builds the house,
　　those who build it labor in vain.
Unless the LORD guards the city,
　　the guard keeps watch in vain.
It is in vain that you rise up early
　　and go late to rest,
eating the bread of anxious toil;
　　for he gives sleep to his beloved.

*Psalm 127:1–2*

The most effective evangelistic pastors hone in with laser-like focus to entice the people they serve to share the faith with new people. These pastors strive, plan and organize with the intensity of the
　　apostle Paul on a mission!
All the while, they are resting in God. They are listening for
　　whispers from the Spirit.

*Martha Grace Reese*

# CHAPTER ONE

# Pastors: Step 1

## *Unbinding the Gospel* with Your Leaders

### Highlights of Chapter 1

- Miracles Require Spiritual Leadership
- First Things First — Your Spiritual Life
- The Secret to Real Life Evangelism — Transformation, Saturation, Momentum
- Identify Your Leaders & Begin a Step 1 Study (20% of worship attendance)
  - Test Balloon with Visionary Leaders
  - Core Leaders
  - Visionary Leaders
  - Church Staff
- The Pastor as Spiritual Leader
- Discern Whether to Move on to Planning for Step 2, the E-vent

The point of the study is to help your leaders become spiritual leaders. We can't just tell people to "go be spiritual." (How has *that* gone in the past?)

### Miracles Require Spiritual Leadership

Do you want change in your church? Have you ever had the sneaking suspicion that real change (well, *good* real changes) would take a *miracle*? You're probably right.

Miracles, true transformation, happen most often when leaders are spiritual leaders. Do you hear the two components to that? The first is "spiritual"; the second is "leader." Real change in churches starts with leadership. Start with your leaders, start with your leaders' spiritual connections with Christ, *if* you want to see shifts toward life, health, deeper spiritual responsiveness to God and systemic changes in your church.

Once your leaders start living the changes, you can move toward a broad-based, all-congregation saturation of the new ideas and habits. We recommend that you train 20% of your average worship attendance during a Step 1 study of *Unbinding the Gospel.* Your true leadership will be ready to share their faith as soon as they are connected with God and see the importance of it. God will reinforce their learning as they teach the rest of the congregation during Step 2, the E-vent.

Miraculous, transformative leadership starts with us, the pastors! The Spirit can use us a lot more easily if we are in love with God and if we're growing, accountable, rested, engaged.

### First Things First

How's your spiritual life? Our research has confirmed a fact that seems so simple, I hesitate to say it out loud. Miraculous, transformative leadership starts with us, the pastors! We must be physically, psychologically and spiritually healthy if we want our congregations to have a chance to flourish. We need to be growing, spiritually and intellectually. I have spelled all of this out in chapter 8 of *Unbinding the Gospel.* Here's the shorthand version: the Spirit can use us a lot more easily if we are in love with God and if we're growing, accountable, rested, engaged.

The flip side of this truth is that we pastors will tend to *stop* authentic movements of the Spirit if we're intellectually or emotionally stagnant; if we're burned out; or if we don't have a vivid, growing relationship with God. God can use us more directly if we're consciously living "in Christ," in the most Pauline sense of that phrase. Can you remember a time when you loved Jesus so much that you prayed for other people to know him, too?

If you aren't in the best spiritual health of your life so far, please start praying and ask God to get you there! Pray with a prayer partner, pray with other pastors in town (*real prayer, not meetings or discussions*). God can restore us to places of spiritual depth that we cannot imagine. Christ can give us vision we never dared hope for, if we *ask* to see, like blind Bartimaeus (Mk. 10:46–52). Will you ask now? Will you yell for healed vision? Will you risk embarrassment? Will you ignore the voices inside and outside your head that tell you to shut up and stop bugging Jesus?

### The Secret to Real Life Evangelism

Your goal is to help God spark interest in evangelism (that is, true faith  and real faith sharing) in your church. Then you work with that little flame until you have long-term, slow-burn momentum in your congregation. Identify and prepare your leaders. You will pray for them and work with them for 8 to 10 weeks. By the end of the *Unbinding the Gospel* study, your leaders should be carrying the process in prayer and bursting with ideas and energy that the Spirit is giving them.

Real life evangelism is a movement of the Spirit. The Spirit moves, then we respond. We can't just hand our leaders a book and tell them to go *do* it. We start by offering ourselves to God to be shaped and transformed as a group of Christians. *This* is what we must offer leaders first — the same thing that is changing our own lives. Our leaders need to experience prayer, not just talk about it. They need to talk about their own faith experiences in small groups. They don't need to *talk about* talking about it!

Some bland "interesting class" or "good program" isn't going to change much. But if your leaders have an experience of God and of actually articulating their faith, they will be ready to lead the whole church into prayer and faith sharing.

### Identify Your Leaders and Begin a Step 1 Study

Every congregation has key leaders. Let's think about three types of important leaders. Let's call them "Visionary Leaders," "Core Leaders," "Enthusiastic Leaders." These categories will merge and overlap, but let's talk simplistically for a moment.

*Try a test balloon with the visionary leaders.* Who are the laypeople to whom you go for sage advice? Which people see issues, dynamics and spiritual realities quickly and clearly? Whom do you trust to read tricky situations? These are your visionary leaders. These are your "quick adapters." Gather them into a small group to do an 8-week, *weekly,* experiential study of *Unbinding the Gospel,* starting the prayer journal the day after you discuss chapter 3.

The more resistant your church tends to be, the more slowly you should move. Start with only one group, if that feels best. Let momentum build slowly, but keep fanning the flames!

*Move on to the core leaders.* When you consider who should be in the group(s) to study *Unbinding the Gospel,* think about the true leaders in your church. Some leaders are "governing leaders,"

> Real life evangelism is a movement of the Spirit. The Spirit moves, then we respond. We can't just hand our leaders a book and tell them to go *do* it. We start by offering ourselves to God to be shaped and transformed as a group of Christians. *This* is what we must offer leaders first — the same thing that is changing our own lives. Our leaders need to experience prayer, not just talk about it.

"spiritual leaders," "core leaders." These leaders serve in different positions in different types of congregations. They may be your elders, deacons, the council, the session, vestry or an *ad hoc* group of key advisors to the pastor. Think about the people who get things done in your church. Think about the people whose opinions, discernment, influence and leadership matter most. Who can stop things from happening? Who can start new projects and keep them moving? These are your core leaders.

*Enthusiastic Leaders.* Enthusiastic leaders are another critically important group of leaders. They're like their name. Who's enthusiastic in your congregation? (Effectively enthusiastic! Remember — we're going for real change, not the congregational equivalent of soap suds.) Who's organized? Who are the inspiring teachers and leaders of your ongoing classes and ministry groups? Who are your spark plugs? Your intercessors? The great youth leaders? The artists? The committed prayer people? Your beloved Sunday school teachers? Who would make a great addition to an evangelism team? (See chapter 10 of *Unbinding the Gospel.*) Who might be terrific leaders for small groups for the all-congregation E-vent? You want to help these folks get involved *now,* so they can help plan and lead the E-vent later. (All three groups of these leaders should make up your 20% of your average worship attendance. Think strategically now!)

*Church staff is crucial.* We learned something important during the Mainline Evangelism Study, as we snooped our way through countless congregations, large and small. Many senior pastors underestimate the crucial importance of the staff. Senior pastors often skimp on team-building, skim through team communication. Pastors can boldly set the direction, fearlessly chart the course, then notice after a while that they've charged off on a walk by themselves. No one's following. That's not so good.

Here's a solution: Pastors, work relationally with your staff team. Lead a study of *Unbinding the Gospel* early in your process. Get each staff member and music director a copy of this book now. Take the time. Do it first. Do it *now. **Please do** it!*

The church staff can determine evangelistic momentum in your congregations. They can help start and sustain movement in a church. They can sabotage change. Work with all the pastors, youth leaders, music directors, administrative assistants, custodians and office workers now! They are the people who will help your congregation change. Or not. Please use this study of ***Unbinding the Gospel*** to build your team. Study it together, as a staff, over time, *before the Step 2, all-congregation E-vent.*

Some bland "interesting class" or "good program" isn't going to change much. But if your leaders have an experience of God and of actually articulating their faith, they will be ready to lead the whole church into prayer and faith sharing.

Some large congregation staffs have chosen to work through *Unbinding the Gospel* weekly for eight to ten weeks during summer or fall, ending with a staff retreat. THEN they are ready to move into leading small groups with their church leaders (Step 1 studies). Your staff will be more likely to be united and in spiritual agreement if you commit to a staff study of **Unbinding the Gospel** (doing the prayer exercises together). The more you talk about these issues and do the exercises together, the more powerfully an E-vent will saturate your church. The dividends of staff spiritual agreement can be enormous.

### The Pastor as Spiritual Leader

Lead a study of **Unbinding the Gospel** with your leaders over a 8- to 10-week period. In medium and large churches you may need two, three, four, 15 study groups — with core leaders, enthusiastic leaders and the church staff. Groups of 8 to 10, with two leaders, are the best size for group dynamics. Here's the key: your personal presence and leadership on any core initiative in your church is irreplaceable, to the extent feasible within your church's size and structure.

*The point of the study is to help your leaders become spiritual leaders*. We can't just tell people to "go be spiritual." (How has *that* gone in the past?) We pastors need to work with leaders in the same way our mentors and the Spirit work with us. If we will be brave enough to walk through experiences with God with the people we serve, Christ will have a much better chance of helping us and our churches become more surrendered, more faithful, more fruitful.

I've found a little quirk in most of us mainline pastors and in the dynamics of most mainline churches. We talk a good game about prayer and faith, but most of us *talk* a lot more about it than we *do* it! We often want to *talk* about prayer, but somehow never get around to praying together. We would rather talk *about* God than do much listening to God. Here's a prediction: both you and your leaders will probably want to talk about God and faith theoretically, but will avoid actually praying together or doing any of the exercises at the ends of the book chapters. We're big talkers. But we need to learn to put our money where our mouths are!

*Do everything you can to share your own faith and to pray together during the course of these studies.*

Ask someone who's more comfortable with the experiential pieces to co-lead the group with you if you're great on the theoretical, terrific at telling-people-stuff, but a little weak on actually praying and talking from your heart. Remember — the goal of the **Unbinding the Gospel** study is to help your core leaders: (a) change their ideas

Here's a prediction: both you and your leaders will probably want to talk about God and faith theoretically, but will avoid actually praying together or doing any of the exercises at the ends of the book chapters. We're big talkers. But we need to learn to put our money where our mouths are!

about evangelism and (b) deepen individual habits of prayer and faith sharing.

Visionary leaders, core leaders, enthusiastic leaders and staff are Step 1. They may be the same people in small congregations. Larger churches have many distinct leadership groups. You will know how to work with your people. Just keep the goal in mind. Get the leaders who can help evangelism (and the leaders who can stop evangelism!) on board. Incorporate leaders and teachers of existing small groups and educational classes during this first stage of the Unbinding the Gospel Series, so that they are committed to the process. If they love **Unbinding the Gospel,** they can lead their own classes in a study of **Unbinding Your Heart** during an E-vent. This provides extraordinary continuity and integration of learning.

*As you lead your study, remember:* Church life can be a spiritual adventure. Our people yearn for an experience of true Christian community, a relationship with God and spiritual excitement. Don't you? Who lusts after tedious meetings and interminable talk?

Remember — the goal of the **Unbinding the Gospel** study is to help your core leaders:

a. change their ideas about evangelism

b. deepen individual habits of prayer and faith sharing

*To help your people launch into a spiritual adventure:*

■ Pray for this process every day. Ask Step 1 group members to commit to pray with you and do the daily prayer exercises in the Prayer Journal. You might also use the *Intercessor's Weekly Prayer List, Prayer Form #33.*

■ Use the discussion questions and work with the exercises in **Gospel** each week. *Or* develop your **own** exercises. Just don't skim over the experiential pieces. Start the *Prayer Journal* the day after your second meeting. Discuss your first completed week of prayer when you talk about chapter 4 on prayer. Don't skimp on time. Pray together as if it mattered. (It does!)

■ Use the suggestions for E-vent small group leaders (see chapter 4 of this book) as you lead your Step 1 study of **Unbinding the Gospel.** You may want to develop a Prayer Team. If so, see chapter 5 for suggestions about how to go about it.

### Discern Whether to Move on to Planning for Step 2, the E-vent

As you and your leaders study **Unbinding the Gospel,** you will all start to sense whether this process is helpful to you. Pray together and discuss whether you should move forward to plan for an E-vent (the all-church study of **Unbinding Your Heart,** the purple ribbon, six-week version of **Unbinding the Gospel,** with individual prayer exercises). You probably have ideas about which of your leaders will do the best job leading small groups, which are great organizers and communicators, who are the natural intercessors. Ask people to begin thinking about their willingness to lead in each of these areas during the E-vent. Pray about pairings of small group leaders.

*Order Unbinding Your Church (this book) for leaders.* If you are going to go ahead with an E-vent, **order copies of *Unbinding Your Church*** well in advance of the first meeting of your E-vent Leadership Team. (See chapter 2.) It is best to pass them out at the first meeting. We recommend that you purchase a copy of **Unbinding Your Church** for each pastor involved in the E-vent, as well as for coordinators of the three teams that will organize the E-vent (the E-vent Team, Small Group Team, and the Prayer Team). You may duplicate sections of the book to make folders/notebooks for every team member, office staff and music staff, under terms of the license agreement on page x at the front of this book. (Chapter 3 details what to put in each group's notebooks. The E-vent Team will be in charge of folder creation.)

Enjoy your **Unbinding the Gospel** study with your leaders. You stand at a choice point. **Decide together:** Do you feel called to move this study into the full congregation? If yes, move on to the next chapter!

> Church life can be a spiritual adventure. Our people yearn for an experience of true Christian community, a relationship with God and spiritual excitement. Don't you? Who lusts after tedious meetings and interminable talk?

### NEWS FLASH!

1. We have discovered that weekly studies of **Unbinding the Gospel** work best. Monthly elders' meetings do not provide the concentration or intensity necessary to produce real change.

2. Don't try to "lead people into" a first GOSPEL study. **NO** preaching or newsletter articles. They only create resistance!

3. Read *Unbinding Your Soul* now — it contains 70 stories and quotes from churches that have done E-vents. It will help you see the trajectory of this process in typical churches.

# CHAPTER TWO

# Pastors: Step 2

## *Unbinding Your Heart* with Your Whole Church

### Highlights of Chapter 2

- What's the E-vent?
- Why *Do* an E-vent@YourChurch?
- Leadership for the E-vent: Three Teams & E-vent Leadership Meetings
  - Pastor, Staff, Youth & Children, Church Musicians (ongoing leadership)
  - E-vent Team (formed for E-vent)
  - Small Group Team (formed for E-vent)
  - Prayer Team (formed for E-vent)
- Order Books
- First E-vent Leadership Team Meeting
- Organize Details — Hand It to God
- Pastors' Charts, Calendars & Forms List

You have finished, or are finishing, your studies of *Unbinding the Gospel.* Have your leaders responded positively? If you all think that it would help your whole congregation, you are ready to move ahead to planning for Step 2 — an all-congregation, small group study of *Unbinding Your Heart: 40 Days of Prayer & Faith Sharing.*

### What's the E-vent?

You have finished, or are finishing, your studies of *Unbinding the Gospel.* Have your leaders responded positively? If you all think that it would help your whole congregation, you are ready to move ahead to planning for Step 2 — an all-congregation, small group study of *Unbinding Your Heart: 40 Days of Prayer & Faith Sharing.*

The E-vent can encompass all facets of your church's life for six weeks. It can be simple or involved. It works with tiny congregations. It works with huge churches.

Planning for the E-vent could be compressed, but we recommend that you go slowly. Take 12 to 16 weeks. All calendars and schedules in this book are premised on a 16-week planning period. Your planning time could begin before Step 1 is finished, if necessary.

### Why _Do_ an E-vent@Your Church?

*The triple focus of the E-vent is why it works.* (1) Individual, (2) small group *and* (3) whole-church saturation of prayer welded to the book's ideas yield results that are greater than the sum of the parts.

The small group experience for each member of the congregation is the keystone of **Unbinding Your Heart.** Daily individual prayer exercises intensify the small group experience. The fact that the whole church is doing the event — in worship, preaching, in small groups and with individual and family prayer — enriches the impact of the E-vent on individuals and in the church.

If you choose to go forward with a typical E-vent, your **church members will:**

- pray individually, daily
- discuss individual prayer with a prayer partner or family members
- meet with their small group, weekly
- worship and pray together as a congregation
- experience sermons, children's sermons, prayers, show-and-tell ("testimonies") from other church members and sing music in sync with each week's **Unbinding Your Heart** theme
- hear members of the church share their faith stories in worship
- participate in all-congregation prayer and faith sharing activities
  - the prayer wall
  - prayer and faith sharing blogs
  - prayer vigil
- read newsletter or e-mail stories from small groups
- attend all-church dinners or "dinners for nine" before their small group gathers
- prepare for a final "invite your friends" celebration a week or two after the end of the E-vent.

> The E-vent can encompass all facets of your church's life for six weeks. It can be simple or involved. It works with tiny congregations. It works with huge churches.

*The point of the E-vent is to anchor new ideas of prayer, faith sharing and rich Christian community in all church members' hearts, souls and habits!*

### Leadership for the E-vent

You have already trained most of the leaders for the E-vent. They're the participants in the *Unbinding the Gospel* study — your visionary leaders, core leaders and enthusiastic leaders. They will help lead in a variety of ways. What will their leadership look like?

*Step 1 participants can all be evangelists for the E-vent. They will help the rest of the congregation get on board.* One goal of the E-vent is to help every small group in the church, every member and every steady visitor to your church experience a six-week, small-group experience in prayer and faith sharing. Your leaders should have gained insights and changed ways of talking and thinking about their faith as they have studied *Unbinding the Gospel.* They will encourage the rest of the congregation to join a small group.

*How can Step 1 participants act as "evangelists for the E-vent"?* They can:

*The triple focus of the E-vent is why it works.* (1) Individual, (2) small group *and* (3) whole-church saturation of prayer welded to the book's ideas yield results that are greater than the sum of the parts.

- Talk with friends.
- Write articles for the newsletter, describing their experience working with *Unbinding the Gospel.*
- Give a short talk during worship services about their Step 1 study, telling how it has been mind-changing and life-changing. Then they can invite the rest of the congregation to join a small group for the E-vent.
- Ask teachers of ongoing groups to participate in the E-vent, even if it means changing their normal schedule. The "E-vent Evangelist" might visit the class the next Sunday, describe the E-vent and ask if the group would be enthusiastic to join in. (If the group leaders were part of a Step 1 study of *Unbinding the Gospel,* this "group recruitment" could happen virtually automatically.)
- Staff a small group sign-up station after worship services, beginning with a "Sign-up Sunday" six weeks before the E-vent starts.

*Background thoughts on forming small groups.* Give existing Sunday school classes and small groups, the choir and worship teams, the junior high and senior high groups the chance to participate in an all-congregation study and prayer experience. Make sure that leaders of all existing groups are a part of the early planning stages of the

E-vent. Changes in existing groups that feel as if they are coming from the "outside" can feel like a threat. (This is the reason we encourage these leaders to take part in a Step 1 study group.)

Try not to ruffle feathers unnecessarily. Remember, not only is change difficult for some, but evangelism itself is a touchy subject in many churches! You may want to lead with the "faith," rather than the "faith *sharing*," aspects! People will get what they need from the book once they start studying it. We're going for creativity and enthusiasm, not resistance! The more choices church leaders and members can exercise, the more "indigenous" the experience, the better.

***Form new groups for the E-vent.*** The E-vent provides a wonderful opportunity for people who are not in a small group to join a new one. People, particularly newer members of churches, tend to be hesitant to take on open-ended commitments. They need small steps. An E-vent study group is only six weeks long. That will help them make friends, but won't lock them in forever. Joining a Sunday school class can feel as daunting to some people as, "Hi! You just became a Christian and joined our church? How'd you like to be chair of our education committee this year?"

How about if we move people in a bit more gradually? An E-vent group shouldn't make anyone grab their Nikes™ and run for the hills. Shall we give it a try?

## **Three E-vent Teams and E-vent Leadership Meetings**

***Teams for the E-vent: Organize — Lead Groups — Pray!*** We suggest that you assemble three teams for the E-vent, in addition to the pastor(s) and representatives from the church's administrative, children and youth, and music ministries. In very small congregations, these "teams" may be a person or two, aided by the church administrative assistant. But whatever your church's size or structure, think in terms of three main "jobs" involved in the E-vent. Members of teams will:

1. plan, organize and communicate the E-vent *(the "E-vent Team," see chapter 3)*

2. lead groups, *(the "Small Group Team," see chapter 4)* and

3. pray and organize prayer opportunities *(the "Prayer Team," see chapter 5)*

***Pastor convenes E-vent leadership meetings.*** As pastor, you will help discern people with gifts for each of the leadership types.

---

The small group experience for each member of the congregation is the keystone of *Unbinding Your Heart.* Daily individual prayer exercises intensify the small group experience. The fact that the whole church is doing the event — in worship, preaching, in small groups and with individual and family prayer — enriches the impact of the E-vent on individuals and in the church.

You will also convene a weekly E-vent meeting. ***Begin early!*** Start meeting 12–16 weeks ***before*** the E-vent starts. Discern who should be the E-vent Coordinator, the Small Group Coordinator, the Prayer Team Coordinator. Invite the coordinators of each of the three teams, together with all pastors working with the E-vent, key office staff, representatives from youth and children's ministries, and the music director. Tailor this group, and its meeting schedule, to fit your church's organization.

The point of the E-vent is to anchor new ideas of prayer, faith sharing and rich Christian community in all church members' hearts, souls and habits!

***Lead E-vent leadership meetings in an "Unbinding" way.*** Please lead E-vent Leadership meetings with the leadership suggestions on page 59 in chapter 4 under the section "All-Leaders' Weekly Meetings." Make prayer a priority. If you structure these meetings around prayer and discernment, your leaders will learn to think in a more Christlike way. They will learn from you how to lead ***their*** teams and small groups. Remember — the E-vent is about prayer and spiritual leadership. The Spirit can work through us best if we leaders are practicing what we preach!

### Order Books

*Order copies of <u>Unbinding Your Church</u>* (pastor's guide, green ribbon) *well in advance* of your first meeting. Pass them out at the first meeting. Purchase a copy of **Unbinding Your Church** for each pastor involved in the E-vent, as well as for coordinators of the three teams (the E-vent Team, Small Group Leaders' Team and the Prayer Team) and your lead musician.

*Unbinding Your Church notebooks for team members.* Your church has permission to copy forms and chapters for team members and your office staff during one E-vent in your own church. Your E-vent Coordinator will be in charge of assembling team members' duplicated, color-coded, team-specific notebooks. Pastors, please double-check that this is done as soon as teams are assembled. (Chapter 3 includes complete instructions for folder contents, assembly and distribution.) For example, each member of the E-vent Team should have a red folder with a copy of the Introduction, chapter 3 and chapter 7 from **Unbinding Your Church,** together with a master list of weekly milestones, a flow chart, meeting schedules and all forms the E-vent Team will use. Your E-vent Coordinator will be in charge of this, but you, as pastor, should double-check to make sure that folders are distributed early.

*Order copies of <u>Unbinding Your Heart: 40 Days of Prayer & Faith Sharing</u> early.* This is the book that the whole congregation will study during the E-event. (It has a purple ribbon on the cover.) The book order is another E-vent Coordinator detail for which you should serve as the double check, fail-safe wing man (or woman)! If you will need *more than **200 copies, order at least 80 percent of them a minimum of eight weeks in advance.*** Please don't be caught short! Order as far ahead of time as possible. See ***www.GraceNet.info*** for up-to-date pricing information and links to suppliers.

### First E-vent Leadership Team Meeting— Prayer, Team Composition, Calendar, Reading Assignment

Begin your planning phase for the E-vent at least 12, preferably 16, weeks before the beginning of your E-vent. You can overlap with your Step 1 studies of **Unbinding the Gospel,** but give your leaders time to decide whether they think an E-vent is the right thing for your church.

Start your first meeting well. Pray together. I suggest that you start every single meeting connected with the E-vent with the same, 10-minute prayer exercise. It's printed in this book in chapter 11

I have included a lot of details and organizational possibilities in the rest of this book. Please remember that those details are merely a structure to carry the Spirit to your people. Your prayer, your yieldingness to God, your ability to listen to the Spirit and to the people you serve are the crucial elements.

*(Praying for Each Other, Prayer Form #36,* p. 129.) The primary goals of your first meeting will be to:

- help your team coordinators come up with lists of enthusiastic, skillful, prayerful, gifted, possible team members
- give other pastors and team coordinators their copies of **Unbinding Your Church** and
- pray for the church.

Your E-vent Leadership Team is your overview team. Think together about who would be great for each of the teams — who prays? Who organizes? Who leads groups well? During your first meeting, come up with a good list of who should be on each team. The team coordinators can meet with people during the next two weeks to ask if they are willing to serve on the teams. As soon as the teams are assembled, they can begin meeting.

*Reading Assignment.* Ask E-vent Leadership Team members to read the introduction, the first two chapters and their "own" chapter by the next meeting. They should read (or at least skim) the whole book by the third meeting. Your E-vent organization will flow more smoothly if everyone knows how they can depend on everyone else.

### Second E-vent Leadership Team Meeting — Pray, Team Recruitment Check-in, Hand out Folders, Discuss *Unbinding Your Church,* Plan Next Steps

First, pray for each other in small groups of three. (Use *Praying for Each Other, Prayer Form #36,* p.129.) Then pray together for the church and your E-vent, for the people God can reach through you.

Your E-vent Team will take responsibility to prepare folders for all E-vent Leadership Team members who do not have a copy of **Unbinding Your Church** in time for your second meeting. (See chapter 3 for details of folder preparation.) The E-vent Team will also have folders to give to team coordinators for each of their team members.

Discuss **Unbinding Your Church**. Go over these notebooks. What do team members think?

From now on, the pastor's job is to inspire, encourage and help keep the Leadership Team's wild creativity on track! Are those "Crazy Kids" making a movie to put on YouTube? Did you and the office staff decide to redesign the worship bulletin to make it more user-friendly to people without a church background? What is the Prayer Team up to?!? Keep that E-vent Leadership Team talking! Don't over-extend, but have fun!

*Everyone:* Keep praying, keep listening, keep thinking, make mid-course adjustments. Have fun!

**NEW** ➡

### Unbinding Your Soul

The E-vent helps us pray and talk about our faith. The Spirit can use it to *create motivation* for faith-sharing and evangelism. NOW help your small groups invite recent visitors and friends who don't go to church into an "experiment in Christianity." *Unbinding Your Soul* is your next step. Please do it quickly! We're seeing that the more immediately small groups move into *SOUL,* the greater the actual, numerical growth.

### Organize Details — Hand It to God

Pastors — I have included a lot of details and organizational possibilities in the rest of this book. Please remember that those details are merely a structure to carry the Spirit to your people. Your prayer, your yieldedness to God, your ability to listen to the Spirit and to the people you serve are the crucial elements.

Here is a little gift, from me! Blessings upon your life, your ministry and your E-vent.

---

## PERMISSION SLIP

_____ *(Fill in your name here)* has full and absolute permission to let something slide.

You may read sermons straight out of ***Unbinding Your Church.***

Punt a newsletter article. Ask someone else to do that hospital visit. Skip a nonessential, or let something slide, ***so long as you spend that time praying.*** With love in Christ,

*Martha Grace Reese*

---

*Pastors:* if you want to pass on this little spark, you could join me in signing permission slips for your leaders. You'll find them on the last pages of chapters 3, 4, 5 and 6! I've already signed them, so if you hate the idea, just snip them out! If you like them, you could sign permission slips for each of the team coordinator's books before you give them out. You could sign slips for the team members' folders. You might choose to give a prayer permission slip like this to everyone in the congregation during worship in week 2, the prayer week. (*Permission Slips, Pastor Forms #9a and #9b*)

*Caveat:* your people may hold you accountable to your own permission slip!

### Pastors' Charts, Calendars & Forms List

(See page 82 for downloading instructions)

- Unbinding the Gospel Series Chart (Sequence of Series) *(Pastor Form #1)*
- Unbinding the Gospel Series Flowchart (How Series Works) *(Pastor Form #2)*
- "Top Ten" E-vent Milestones *(Pastor Form #3)*
- E-vent Leadership Team Diagram *(Pastor Form #4)*
- E-vent Leadership Team Roster *(Pastor Form #5)*
- E-vent Leadership Team Meeting Schedule *(Pastor Form #6)*
- Pastor's E-vent Worship Calendar *(Pastor Form #7)*
- Pastor's "E-vent Evangelists" Recruitment (newsletter articles and "Show & Tell") *(Pastor Form #8)*
- Permission Slips *(Pastor Forms #9a and #9b)*
- Pastor's Weekly Checklist *(Pastor Form #9c)*

# CHAPTER THREE

# The E-vent Team

## Highlights of Chapter 3

- The Goal of the E-vent and the Means of Reaching It
- Your E-vent Team & E-vent Coordinator
- Assemble and Distribute Folders
- E-vent Small Groups — Formation & Organization
  - Overview
  - Help from the Small Group Team
  - Existing Groups
  - Form New Small Groups for the E-vent
- Choice Points as You Form Small Groups
- Small Group Assignments
- Small Group Member Roster (the Master List)
- Order Books
- An E-vent Celebration — Want to Give a Party?
- List of E-vent Team's Forms

The *main goal of the E-vent* is to help your church (and each person in your church) grow closer to God and begin to share their faith. Here's another way of saying it: the goal of the E-vent is to help people to change their ideas about prayer and evangelism, and to begin to practice new, healthy habits of prayer and faith sharing.

### The Goal of the E-vent and the Means of Reaching It

The *main goal of the E-vent* is to help your church (and each person in your church) grow closer to God and begin to share their faith. Here's another way of saying it: the goal of the E-vent is to help people to change their ideas about prayer and evangelism, and to begin to practice new, healthy habits of prayer and faith sharing.

The *means of reaching the E-vent's goal* is to ask all members and regular visitors of your church to

**37**

- participate fully in a weekly small group that studies **Unbinding Your Heart**
- pray for 40 days, using **Unbinding Your Heart**'s individual prayer exercises and
- participate in worship and all church activities that reinforce each week's study of **Unbinding Your Heart**.

### Your E-vent Team & E-vent Coordinator

*E-vent Team — Organizers and Communicators*. Your E-vent Team and your *E-vent Coordinator* will oversee the details of planning for the E-vent. They will also be charged with communications — through letters, newsletters, e-mails, list-serves, Web site, blogs, carrier pigeons — whatever they come up with!

*Qualities of the E-vent Coordinator?* The E-vent Coordinator could be a staff person (an associate pastor, an administrator, an office staff member), or a layperson with great organizational gifts. Look for someone who is enthusiastic and organized. Team members should be people with specific gifts in the E-team's areas: organization, communications, a great phone talker, wonderful writers and people with Internet and technical skills. *E-vent Team Members*. E-vent Coordinator — recruit your E-vent Team early! Discuss possible members at your first meeting(s) of the E-vent Leadership Team. Begin to meet with your team. Pray together from the very beginning. I suggest that you all start every meeting connected with the E-vent with ten minutes of praying together in a specific way. I have written out instructions that you'll find on *Prayer Form #36*, p. 129. Remember: the Spirit can infuse your group. The Spirit will lead you, *if* you will listen. Could you think of this team as your small group for the time you're together? That is how all church meetings can be. Don't just be task doers! Pray for each other and pray for guidance about what Christ can do through your team.

*Small churches*. Please don't let all these ridiculous details overwhelm you! You know your church. Pray about the suggestions. The only essentials are the Essentials! (See the introduction.) We do an E-vent to help people pray and talk with each other. We don't want the E-vent to feel like someone's loading more bricks in your backpack! Select the few things that you can do well and comfortably from that long row of cafeteria options. Everyone doesn't need to eat barbecue *and* chicken *and* fish *and* a fajita!

The Spirit can infuse your group. The Spirit will lead you, *if* you will listen. Could you think of this team as your small group for the time you're together? That is how all church meetings can be. Don't just be task doers! Pray for each other and pray for guidance about what Christ can do through your team.

## What Can the E-vent Team Do?

We see the E-vent Team coordinating these types of activities:

- Assemble folders for all E-vent leaders
- Organize as many people in the congregation as possible into small groups. (The Small Group Team will help.)
  - Work with existing groups to coordinate study of ***Unbinding Your Heart***
  - Enlist new members in new small groups formed for the E-vent
- Coordinate people's schedules, assign group times and meeting rooms (work with office staff)
- Order books (coordinate this with the pastor)
- Be the E-vent Communications Nerve Center (coordinate with office staff)
  - Newsletter
  - Special mailings
  - E-mail
  - Posters and signs around church
  - Web site, Web-based discussion groups and blogs
  - You really don't have to do carrier pigeons, but doesn't it sound like a fun youth activity?
- Coordinate information, lists & rosters with Small Group Leaders, the Prayer Team, the pastor and office staff
- Coordinate details for common meals during the E-vent, if you chose to offer them
- Organize and publicize an "invite-your-friends" celebration to be given a week or two after the E-vent ends — Palm Sunday, then a luncheon? the First Sunday of Advent, then lunch? a December luncheon with Christmas carols? an Easter Egg hunt? a Habitat project or local mission event? Large churches might do several of these options.

*Small churches.* Please don't let all these ridiculous details overwhelm you! You know your church. Pray about the suggestions. The only essentials are the Essentials! We do an E-vent to help people pray and talk with each other. We don't want the E-vent to feel like someone's loading more bricks in your backpack! Select the few things that you can do well and comfortably from that long row of cafeteria options. Everyone doesn't need to eat barbecue *and* chicken *and* fish *and* a fajita.

## Assemble and Distribute Folders

The E-vent Team's first big job is to assemble folders for everyone who's leading in the E-vent. The office staff will help. Things will go much more smoothly if you: (a) assemble the folders early (make extras for latecomers), and (b) help keep contents updated as your E-vent planning goes on. Lists will change.

*Coordinator:* check at every E-vent Leadership Team Meeting to make sure that you have the latest lists and information. The list of weekly milestones, schedules and rosters will change, so update it when you need to. (Make sure to date every document you touch! It may help to copy updated replacements on different colored paper.) Then distribute the new data for people to keep in their folders.

Everyone will thank you. At least they **should** thank you. If they don't, they're just being rude.

*Assemble and hand out folders to team coordinators (one for each member of their teams, plus a couple of extras for latecomers) at the second E-vent Leadership Team meeting.* Please give people everything you can as soon as possible. Rosters and schedules will take a while. Don't wait for them! Distribute folders with at least the charts, diagrams, general information, and the chapters from *Unbinding Your Church* as soon as possible. See if you can give folders to all the team coordinators at the E-vent Leadership Meeting before their groups meet for the first time. You would be heroes if the team leaders (E-vent, Prayer, Small Group, Children & Youth) could pass out folders to their brand new team members at their first meetings.

Give them new or updated, hole-punched documents as you get them! This will help team members begin to feel organized, prepared and committed to the planning process. The E-vent Coordinator will probably be passing out revised lists at nearly every E-vent Leadership Team meeting. *General Rule: Give everyone organized, updated, dated information as soon as you have it.*

*Color Coding.* We have assigned a special color to each group involved in the E-vent planning. For example, the Prayer Team is purple. The E-vent Team is red. Pastors are blue. We encoded each of the forms you can download from the Web site (*see chapter 11*) with the responsible group's color. You'll help everyone if you get folders that match each group's color, too. The best idea is to get folders that accept 3–hole-punched papers. Make sure they also have side pockets for loose documents and notes.

*Make Extra Folders.* As you decide numbers of folders, make up two or three extra folder sets for each of the teams. Teams may add members. Someone could lose a folder. It's easier to make a few extras at the beginning than to go back and reconstruct!

*Folder Contents.* Folders will have documents in common as well as documents that are just for that group. Here are our ideas of what will help your teams. We have put most forms online so that we could add color and make them larger for you. Here are two lists.

## Assemble and Distribute Folders

The E-vent Team's first big job is to assemble folders for everyone who's leading in the E-vent. The office staff will help. Things will go much more smoothly if you: (a) assemble the folders early (make extras for latecomers), and (b) help keep contents updated as your E-vent Planning goes on. Lists will change.

Items in the first list go in all folders. The second list is group-specific. Adjust as necessary:

### List 1: Items for every folder

- Unbinding the Gospel Series Chart, Sequence of Series (*Pastor Form #1*, page 7).
- Unbinding the Gospel Series Flowchart (How the Series Works), *Pastor Form #2* (See a gray tone version on page 16. If you have access to a color printer/copier, please use the Web site version. It's **gorgeous**!)
- "Top Ten" Event Milestones *(Pastor Form #3)*
- E-vent Leadership Team Diagram *(Pastor Form #4)*
- All Rosters of Teams & Groups (these will be added to and revised as the planning period goes on)
- Introduction, **Unbinding Your Church**
- Chapter 7, **Unbinding Your Church**
- Your church's particular info (calendar, newsletter submission schedules, whatever else you think they need)

### List 2: Here is a chart of the contents of the folders that will change for each group.

#### Group-Specific Items for Folders

| Team | Color | Chapter | Mtg Schedules | # of Copies | Forms |
|---|---|---|---|---|---|
| Office Staff | green | 1, 2, 3, 7 | all meetings | ___ + 1 | All |
| All Pastors | blue | Buy books | all meetings | ___ | All |
| 3 Team Coordinators | team's color | Buy books | all meetings | 3 | All |
| Music Director | gray | 8, 9, 10 | Leadership | 1 | |
| E-vent Team (E-V) | red | 3 | E-vent | ___ + 2/3 | No. 10 - 19 |
| Small Group Team (SG) | orange | 3, 4* | Groups | ___ + 2/3 | No. 20 - 25 |
| Prayer Team | purple | 5, 7 | Prayer | ___ + 2/3 | No. 30 - 37 |

Coordinator: check at every E-vent Leadership Team Meeting to make sure that you have the latest lists and information. The list of weekly milestones, schedules and rosters will change, so update it when you need to. (Make sure to date every document you touch! It may help to copy updated replacements on different colored paper.) Then distribute the new data for people to keep in their folders.

---

*Give chapters 3 and 4 to the Small Group Team members. Copy just chapter 4 for the Small Group Leaders' packets.

Your organization will help everyone! Coordinator: remember to check for changes, keep lists updated (and dated). Keep the information flow going!

### E-vent Small Groups — Formation & Organization

***Organizing the Small Groups: The BIG Job!*** Folders are a fun, artworky, organizational task that will help everyone do their jobs. But the ***biggest, BEST*** job lies ahead! You get to help everyone in your church learn of, get excited about, and commit to the E-vent! The E-vent Team is in charge of getting everyone signed up for a small group. You are in charge of organizing and scheduling the small groups. Do you like jigsaw puzzles? Then you are going to have ***so*** much fun!

### Overview of Organizing Small Groups

Think of the process of organizing small groups as being like sand going into the top of an hourglass, and flowing out. (Don't worry, you don't have to have a green-faced witch cackling beside you.) Information, lists, people's preferences, details about scheduling, rooms, who needs childcare, leaders, existing groups all funnel to you, the E-vent Team.

You all sit at the waist of the hourglass; you sort the information, figure out how everything fits together (do your jigsaw puzzle). Then, send out your organized rosters and schedules. Check with meal and childcare providers, order and distribute books. Fire your starter's pistol. The E-vent begins…!

> But the ***biggest, BEST*** job lies ahead! You get to help everyone in your church learn of, get excited about, and commit to the E-vent! The E-vent Team is in charge of getting everyone signed up for a small group. You are in charge of organizing and scheduling the small groups. Do you like jigsaw puzzles? Then you are going to have so much fun!

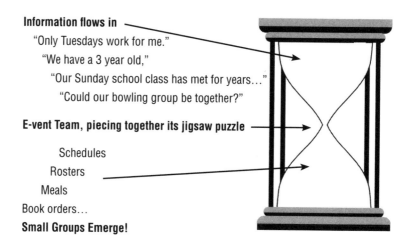

**Information flows in**
"Only Tuesdays work for me."
"We have a 3 year old,"
"Our Sunday school class has met for years…"
"Could our bowling group be together?"

**E-vent Team, piecing together its jigsaw puzzle**

Schedules
Rosters
Meals
Book orders…
**Small Groups Emerge!**

*In other words, here's the big picture:*

> You tell people about the E-vent.
>   You collect information.
>     You sort it.
>   You come up with groups.
> You tell everyone the plan.

Start early. Take your time. Use whatever organizing techniques you think will work for your church.

We've come up with some that we think will be helpful for a lot of churches. You decide, adapt, adopt, or pitch. Just keep organized and have fun!

*****

*Your goal is to help everyone in the congregation into an E-vent group so that they can study Unbinding Your Heart for six weeks.*

## Sources for Group Participants

Four sources, or "waves" can fill your groups. Let all four waves wash through and fill up your groups. Saturate your congregation with information and opportunities to sign up.

1. *Existing classes and groups* study *Unbinding Your Heart* (*Groups Form #22*)

2. *New small group leaders recruit the core of their own groups* — friends, neighbors, colleagues (*E-vent Form #12*)

3. *General, "y'all come" sign-up for small groups* that kicks off official registration season. Your pastor preaches an introductory sermon on Sign-up

4. *Last minute recruits* through 2nd week of study (Web, newsletter, worship bulletin inserts, phone calls ("wait...Can I still sign up for that thing?" "Could my neighbor come?" "I just...")

## Enrolling Group Members

*Keep the big picture in mind — help everyone in the church sign up to be part of a small group.*

All the decisions and choices flow from that. You collect as much information about as many groups and people as you can. You sift and sort. Sand in...sand out. Then people are in groups, and the E-vent starts. Be creative and keep at it. It'll be great!

> Think of the process of organizing small groups as being like sand going into the top of an hourglass, and flowing out. (Don't worry, you don't have to have a green-faced witch cackling beside you.) Information, lists, people's preferences, details about scheduling, rooms, who needs childcare, leaders, existing groups all funnel to you, the E-vent Team.

### The Enrollment Process

*1. Sunday, six weeks before E-vent starts...*

▪ Post specific group sign-up lists *(E-vent Form #12)*.

▪ Recruit at "E-vent Table" after worship *(E-vent Form #13)*.

▪ Distribute sign-up forms through Web, newsletter, worship bulletin, e-mail, letter invitation *(E-vent Form #13)*.

*2. Help from the Small Group Team*

▪ They will recruit & train the Small Group Leaders.

▪ The pastor(s) and the Small Group Team will discern whom to ask to lead your E-vent small groups. The Small Groups Coordinator and members of the Groups Team will speak with these potential leaders to see if they are willing to lead groups and to discover their schedule preferences. The Small Group Team will give the E-vent Team completed rosters that have names and contact information for both leaders and all members of existing groups *(Groups Form #22)*. They will also give you rosters of names and contact information for people who have agreed to lead new small groups *(Groups Form #23)*. The new small groups will not have member names. The E-vent Team will do that part!

*3. The main division of labor for group formation is:*

▪ The Small Group Team will be the primary leaders/servers for the leaders, the content of what they're teaching, and the ways they teach.

▪ The E-vent team organizes people into groups and orchestrates communication about all aspects of the E-vent.

*4. Where do small groups come from?*

▪ The existing groups will be handed to you by the Small Group Team. (You all, of course, will have been doing terrific communication about the E-vent, to help existing groups leap onto the band wagon!) The rest of the small groups burst into being as everyone else in the congregation races to sign up to be in a new group formed for the E-vent. You all will be giving them many reasons, in many ways, why the E-vent is going to be fabulous. That will help people gain momentum for all the leaping, bursting and racing.

*5. Form new groups for the E-vent*

▪ Ask everyone who is not part of a study class or group if they would be willing to join a six-week, E-vent small group

---

You all sit at the waist of the hourglass; you sort the information, figure out how everything fits together (do your jigsaw puzzle). Then, send out your organized rosters and schedules. Check with meal and childcare providers, order and distribute books. Fire your starter's pistol. The E-vent begins...!

adventure! Try to think of effective layers of communication/ invitation that will fit your church. You have already spoken with leaders of existing groups, so many people will already be committed to the E-vent. What about the rest?

### Types of Information

Offer as many types of information and invitations as you can. The more people involved, the more venues, the more modes of communication, the greater the success in attracting virtually everyone in your church into enthusiastic participation in a small group. You will need general announcements. You'll also want to follow up with relational, personal contacts. Using many ways to sign-up for groups can seem chaotic, but seems to yield better results. Here are a few of many possibilities:

*General Rule:* Give everyone organized, updated, ***dated*** information as soon as you have it.

*1. **Publish information** and "testimonies" about the E-vent in the church newsletter, in e-mails to all members, on the church Web site and in worship bulletins, starting eight to ten weeks before the E-vent.

*2. **Unbinding the Gospel Alumni—your "E-vent Evangelists!"*** Some of your most influential church leaders already have a deep understanding of and commitment to the upcoming E-vent. They have studied **Unbinding the Gospel**. They populate the event planning teams! Ask them to…

- write articles for the newsletter or Web site
- give short talks in worship
- talk with their friends; and
- speak to existing groups and classes in church.

*3. **Ask leaders of existing groups to talk with their own members about the E-vent.*** Encourage them to explain the E-vent (with the help of an E-vent Evangelist, preferably from the group itself), then enroll their members for the study. (*Use Groups Form #22.*)

*4. **Some churches encourage the Small Group Leaders to recruit their own groups.*** They can start as soon as they know that they will be leading a group. The more people who recruit their friends, the better. Encourage leaders to include unchurched friends. (*Use E-vent Form #12.*)

*5. **"Sign-Up Sunday!" The pastor can give a blockbuster introductory sermon.*** Six weeks before the E-vent starts, your pastor can describe the E-vent. S/he'll invite everyone to participate through worship, in their private prayer lives, and in a small group. (*See Part II of this book for music, worship and sermon resources.*)

The E-vent Coordinator is in charge of ordering copies of *Unbinding Your Heart: 40 Days of Prayer & Faith Sharing* (purple ribbon) at least a month in advance. We recommend that you estimate the number of books you'll need, then *add a 5% cushion* for late registrants.

*6. E-vent Sign-up Station.* Have a table outside the sanctuary or in the Fellowship Hall after worship each week starting with Sign-up Sunday. Staff it with an *Unbinding the Gospel* Alum!

*7. Make sign-up forms available through various sources.* Make sure every newsletter, e-mail communication and worship bulletin, beginning with introductory Sermon Sunday, contains an individual sign-up form. (*E-vent Form #13*)

*8. Pray about possibilities.* Be creative! Talk with natural leaders of groups of friends about whether they might be interested in leading a group. It's only for six weeks!

*9. Make follow-up phone calls* to anyone in the church who has not signed up for a group yet. Include visitors! Begin calling two or three weeks before the E-vent starts.

### Choice Points as You Form Small Groups

Here are choices the E-vent Committee needs to consider and decide early:

*1. Childcare?* Will you offer childcare? Have you ever been a parent of small children? Do you remember the relief when someone *else* was organizing childcare and taking care of them for a bit? Keep those tired parents in mind as you plan! Perhaps your can organize a young mom's exercise/study small group during school hours, and provide childcare for little children and infants. What about a parents' small group during Sunday school hour? We strongly urge that you arrange for childcare for groups that need it. (All sign-up forms include a childcare request. Use *E-vent Form #15* to actually schedule the childcare!)

*2. Cost?* Be sure to include cost information on each sign-up form. We have included a space for this. Some churches may give out books free. (It may be best to give everyone a book without charge, but include an envelope with a letter in the book, describing that the book is a gift. Say that it cost $_____ per copy, and that people can contribute in the envelope.)

*3. When to meet? Meals?* Some churches schedule most of their small groups at the church on a specific night. They share a meal before small group time. It's easier to talk and pray with people with whom you've just shared a fun dinner. A common meal also makes family and childcare arrangements easier. *(See E-vent Form #16 for a Meal Preparation Schedule.)* Other churches arrange dinners for 9 or 12 in people's homes. These numbers work well since ***Unbinding Your Heart's*** exercises often ask people to talk and pray in groups of three. Some groups meet over breakfast, before work, downtown, or after an exercise class. It's important to have a private room so that groups can pray. Be very flexible. Let groups of people form creatively.

***4. Late group joiners.*** Ask the Small Group Leaders if they are comfortable with late joiners to their group. Some congregations may choose to allow people to join groups as late as the beginning of the third week of the study. Just be clear! You might choose to form a "late-comers' group" rather than try to integrate people into groups that have already started. Let the Small Group Leaders make this call.

***5. Web-based communication?*** If you have a good Web master, will you set up a blog:

- to talk about how daily prayer exercises are going
- for intercession (you could use a photo of your Prayer Wall)
- for discussions between members of different small groups about prayer
- for faith-sharing and what they're learning?

### Small Group Assignments — Taming the Chaos!!

The E-vent Team will sit, with little slips of paper flying around the room like leaves twirling in fall wind. It's four weeks before the E-vent. A few team members are wishing they had taken their vacations right now, but the die-hard organizers are grinning! This is when it gets great. This is jigsaw puzzle time, when the tough get going. You guys know what to do. Figure out who can meet when. See which rooms fit. Get the times straight. Who needs childcare? Come up with your first, tentative, nonpublic roster.

### Sand Is Streaming into the Bottom of the Hourglass — Time to Distribute Your Small Group Member Roster (the Master List)!

Next week, when you have more sign-up sheets, do a little more. Keep adding names, keep forming groups, keep replacing the roster until the very end. We have made a Small Group Member Roster (Master List) *(E-vent Form #14)*. Most churches will want to keep the roster on the computer, but *E-vent Form #14* will give you the categories you don't want to miss. We recommend that you have

> If you need **MORE THAN 200 COPIES of Unbinding Your Heart,** estimate the number of copies you'll need and order at least 80% of that number **EIGHT WEEKS IN ADVANCE.**

only one, huge, compendium, summary roster with all the groups, all the meeting times and places, all the leaders, all the members, all the contact information.

Remember to date revised rosters. We always recommend using a new paper color for revisions.

Distribute the list to all members of the E-vent Leadership Team. Give them copies for their team members. This will get the lists to the office staff, the small group leaders and the prayer team.

### Order Books — Unbinding Your Heart

**Throw a Party!**

Remember: fun, low stress, low pressure and moral support! We're inviting our friends to a first taste of the greatest party ever given — our church!

*The E-vent Coordinator is in charge of ordering copies of* **Unbinding Your Heart: 40 Days of Prayer & Faith Sharing** (purple ribbon) *at least a month in advance*. We recommend that you estimate the number of books you'll need, then *add a 5% cushion* for late registrants.

*If you need MORE THAN 200 COPIES, estimate the number of copies you'll need and order at least 80% of that number EIGHT WEEKS IN ADVANCE.* (Special discounts for advance orders and large quantities are available. See *www.GraceNet.info* for up-to-date pricing and ordering information).

*Coordinator:* Go over this book order in your E-vent Leadership Team meeting and consult with the pastor, but you are in charge. Please, please *order enough copies in advance*! All sorts of things can slow down book orders, so plan ahead and order early. You don't want to do all this work and be caught in a panic at the end.

### An E-vent Celebration—Want to Give a Party?

Two important things can happen in your church during the E-vent. First, your members can connect more deeply with God and learn to talk about their faith. Second, it can lead to people:

- inviting their friends to church, and
- talking about their faith in the World Outside Church!

The E-vent can help everyone practice both parts in the least threatening way possible. Studying *Unbinding Your Heart* will get them started on deepening their faith and talking about it. You, the E-vent Team, can help them practice the inviting-people-to-church part by giving everyone a chance to invite friends to church at the same time. (Provide a little moral support!)

### Timing for the Celebration

Chose a time a week or two after the end of the E-vent.

Make it a party, a big celebration with a meal, an activity with some faith component. It could be a special worship service (1st Sunday of Advent, Palm Sunday, Easter, first "welcome back" day of fall), a big kids' event, a service project, a Christmas luncheon with a talk on prayer.

### Begin Early

Let your members know you will have a special event to which everyone is encouraged to invite friends. Ask them to ask God whom they should invite. Ask if they will pray for that person before issuing an invitation. It helps people to have a written invitation to hand people. *(See E-vent Form #17 for a sample invitation.)* Ask the children and youth leaders to help plan great stuff for the kids' friends, too!

Remember: fun, low stress, low pressure and moral support! We're inviting our friends to a first taste of the greatest party ever given — our church!

### Unbinding Your Soul  NEW

The E-vent helps us pray and talk about our faith. The Spirit can use it to *create motivation* for faith-sharing and evangelism. NOW help your small groups invite recent visitors and friends who don't go to church into an "experiment in Christianity." *Unbinding Your Soul* is your next step. Please do it quickly! We're seeing that the more immediately small groups move into *SOUL,* the greater the actual, numerical growth.

### To You, Wonderful E-vent Team!

The E-vent Team has an exciting challenge. Be as creative and flexible as possible **and** stay compulsively organized! And now, dear E-vent Team members, here is a Permission Slip for you. You are the conscientious ones. Have fun with the E-vent! Unclench that jaw! Ask for help when you need it!

The larger the church, the more complex the organization of the E-vent. But, the larger the church, the more familiar you will be with large-scale planning and communicating. The E-vent Team has an exciting challenge. Be as creative and flexible as possible **and** stay compulsively organized!

```
┌ ─ ─ ─ ─ ─ ─ ─ ─ ─ ─ ─ ─ ─ ─ ─ ─ ┐
```

### PERMISSION SLIP

_____ *(Fill in your name*

*here)* has full and absolute permission to let something slide.

Leave the bed unmade. Postpone laundry. Let that grass grow.

Don't make that last E-vent phone call. Change the oil in the car

next week. Ask for help instead of doing everything yourself!

Take a morning off, drink tea and look out the window. You

may skip a job. You may let something slide *so long as you*

*spend that time praying.*

With love in Christ,

*Martha Grace Reese*          _____

Pastor's Signature

```
└ ─ ─ ─ ─ ─ ─ ─ ─ ─ ─ ─ ─ ─ ─ ─ ─ ┘
```

### E-vent Team Forms

(See page 82 for downloading instructions)

- E-vent Team Member Roster *(E-vent Form #10)*
- E-vent Team Meeting Schedule *(E-vent Form #11)*
- Small Group Leader & Member Roster, Existing Groups *(Groups Form #22)*
- Small Group Leader Roster, New Groups *(Groups Form #23)*
- Sign up to Join an E-vent Small Group! (Posted Version for Bulletin Boards) *(E-vent Form #12)*
- Sign up to Join an E-vent Small Group! (Newsletter, Worship Insert, Hand-out, E-mail, Web version) *(E-vent Form #13)*
- Small Group Member Roster (Master List) *(E-vent Form #14)*
- Childcare Schedule *(E-vent Form #15)*
- Meal Preparation Schedule *(E-vent Form #16)*
- Sample Invitation *(E-vent Form #17)*
- ***Unbinding Your Heart*** Book Order Form *(E-vent Form #18)*
- E-vent Team Weekly Checklist *(E-vent Form #19)*

# CHAPTER FOUR

# The Small Group Team

**Highlights of Chapter 4**

*Part I — The Small Group Team*

- The First Job: Choose Small Group Leaders
- Your Step 1 Study: It's Leader Training…and Recruitment!
- Existing Groups Become E-vent Groups

*Part II — Small Group Leaders*

- How to Lead an E-vent Group
- Good Group Dynamics Rules
- *Unbinding the Gospel* compared to *Unbinding Your Heart*
- All-Leaders Weekly Meetings
- Small Group Team Forms List

### PART I —The Small Group Team

*The Small Group Team does two main things:*

1. You will figure out who the very best teachers/small group leaders are and ask them to lead a group during the E-vent.

2. Then you get to facilitate a weekly group for these leaders/teachers.

You get to serve on the Small Group Team? You are so blessed! You will be living in the middle of the action. The Small Group Team does two main things. (1) You will figure out who the very best teachers/small group leaders are and ask them to lead a group during the E-vent. (2) Then you get to facilitate a weekly group for these leaders/teachers.

*Your Small Group Team consists of a Small Group Coordinator and three or four members* (adjust this for the size of your church). By a month before the E-vent itself, your team's focus will shift from organizing to preparing for the actual leading of groups. The Small

Group Team will grow to include all of the group leaders at that point. The original, small, organizing Team can function as an "executive" group, and as the "leaders of leaders" for the full group.

Tell the E-vent Coordinator that everyone, all the leaders as well as the original organizing team, will need a folder!

Your ***Small Group Coordinator*** should be great with people, and a terrific organizer. S/he will herd you during meetings, even if it's like herding cats. S/he will keep details and lists organized. During the E-vent itself, your team will lead small groups of small group leaders in weekly prayer/discussion/processing meetings.

You, the executive group, will give the leaders their ***own*** small group experience. You'll help the leaders work through the glitches, you'll applaud their successes and growth, you'll facilitate the leaders' prayers. Help them feel that someone has their backs. Let the small group leaders know that you're in their corner, that their own leaders' group is there to pray for them, and to help them lead well. Your small group leaders will be able to pass on something of the depth and quality of this experience.

Add their gifts and graces to the mix. Then watch what God can do with these small groups in people's lives!

This chapter deals with two main issues:

■ Choosing leaders for small groups and asking them to serve
■ Practical advice for how to lead a small group for the E-vent (This advice should be helpful to both the Small Group Team leading the leaders, and to the small group leaders as they lead their groups during the E-vent.)

#### The First Job — Choose Small Group Leaders

The Small Group Team is responsible for finding leaders for groups. You will have help. The pastor(s) and the E-vent Leadership Team will go over ideas of who would be best to help organize the E-vent, to be part of the Prayer Team, to organize some dinners, to work with kids and to lead groups. But after they have thought about it in the E-vent Leadership Team, you all will discern who to ask to lead groups.

*Small Group Coordinator:* please read chapter 3, the E-vent Team chapter. Your two teams have overlapping responsibilities for small groups, so chapter 3 contains quite a bit about small groups.

Small group leaders come in two forms! First, people are already leading groups and teaching classes in your church. Their groups/

*You, the executive group, will give the leaders their own small group experience. You'll help the leaders work through the glitches, you'll applaud their successes and growth, you'll facilitate the leaders' prayers. Help them feel that someone has their backs. Let the small group leaders know that you're in their corner, that their own leaders' group is there to pray for them and to help them lead well. Your small group leaders will be able to pass on something of the depth and quality of this experience.*

classes can become E-vent small groups. Second, you can recruit new leaders for small groups formed especially for the E-vent.

Talk about this. Read this whole chapter before you ask anyone to lead a group! Can you see pictures in your head of the types of people who can lead one of these groups best? Small groups flourish with good facilitators. You are looking for leaders who will help other people think, talk and pray in an atmosphere of respect and safety.

### Your Step 1 Study of *Unbinding the Gospel* — It's Leader Training...and Recruitment!

Gilda Radner and Dan Ackroyd did an old *Saturday Night* live skit, an advertisement for "Shimmer" — a brand new product in an aerosol can. In my memory of it, Gilda mopped her kitchen floor, "I love this new floor wax." Dan Ackroyd took the can from her, "No dear, it's a dessert topping!"…"Huh-*uh*, sweetheart. It's a floor wax!!!" (She mopped with it, smiling maniacally.) "Dearest, it's a ***dessert*** topping." (He ate some on pudding). "Voiceover: "No, you silly kids! It's ***both***! Shimmer is a floor wax ***and*** a dessert topping."

Okay. So think about it. Your church's leaders just studied ***Unbinding the Gospel***. It was a study. No, it was leader training and recruitment for the E-vent. *No*, it was a small group study of evangelism and prayer. ***Nooooo***, it was leader training and recruitment for the E-vent. Ohhhhhh, you silly kids — it was ***both****!*

If you have finished (or nearly finished) your church's study of ***Unbinding the Gospel***, your church has already trained 20% of its leaders to teach, pray, plan and lead the E-vent. Your church's core leaders, visionary leaders and enthusiastic leaders are already excited about doing the E-vent, or you wouldn't be reading this! You've already decided, together, to do the all-congregational study. Your leaders are essentially trained, if your small groups really talked, prayed and did the exercises in your Step 1 study.

So, look at the list of people who have already studied ***Unbinding the Gospel***. Who already leads a group? (We're talking about ***any*** kind of group — a study group, the Habitat team, the 20-year-olds who work on cars for single moms, the gourmet group, the Pilates class, the lawn mowing crew.) Now think about who would be a great group leader for a new group. Those are your core people.

First — work with the leaders of your church's existing groups. Second — ask new leaders. Does anyone now strike you as a natural group leader, who might not have taken part in a small group study (and teacher training!) of *Unbinding the Gospel?* It you follow our recommendation, and begin asking people to be teachers 12 weeks before the start of the E-vent, you could do a special "It's a Study Group — It's Teacher Training!" group/training for the people you'd love to see lead a group during the E-vent.

### Existing Groups Become E-vent Groups

Estimate the number of groups your church will form. Your best estimate is to divide average worship attendance by 12, or 13 or 14. Use the adult worship attendance figure — the youth and children leaders will be the leaders for the junior and senior high groups. Our goal is for every active participant in the congregation to be in a small group for the E-vent. Every person may not join, but we will encourage all of our members and our small group leaders to invite their unchurched friends and neighbors into a group. What a wonderful way to get to know a church well!

You'll need fewer groups if you have large Sunday school classes that have decided to study the book together. Ask all leaders of existing study groups if they will be part of the E-vent. Think about Sunday school classes, small groups, women's and men's groups, mission and service groups, the youth groups from junior high and older.

Optimal group size is 10 people with two leaders. Existing groups that use a lecture format may be much larger than 10. Ask leaders if they would like to split up into small groups for the E-vent. This is completely voluntary. Let it be a question for the normal teachers' consideration, not a requirement! However, if all teachers were included in the Step 1 study of *Unbinding the Gospel*, they will probably be enthusiastic about participating. They should also have a deep appreciation of the small group format. Some existing groups may decide to suspend their normal meeting schedule and encourage all of their members to join a specially formed, new "E-vent" small group.

You could ask "E-vent Evangelists" to speak with existing groups. (See chapter 2.) The E-vent Leadership Team should consider various existing groups and add any wisdom. Decide who should speak with group leaders.

When existing groups decide that they want to be part of the E-vent as an ongoing group, help their leader(s) fill in a Small Group Leader & Member Roster for Existing Groups *(Groups Form #22)*. Then give copies of these completed forms to the E-vent Team.

---

**Sidebar:**

When existing groups decide that they want to be part of the E-vent as an ongoing group, help their leader(s) fill in a Small Group Leader & Member Roster for Existing Groups (Groups Form #22). Then give copies of these completed forms to the E-vent Team.

Please get two leaders for each new small group you are planning. The optimal size for a group is 8–10 participants. It's better to start with groups of 10, in case you lose a person or two over the course of the E-vent. When people have agreed to serve as leaders, please enter their names and contact information on the Small Group Leader Roster for New Groups *(Groups Form #23)*. A copy of these rosters goes to the E-vent Team as soon as possible.

### PART II — Small Group Leaders

You have said "yes" to serving as a leader. Thank you. Your church and the other leaders will help you co-lead your small group during the E-vent. Talk with each other about your questions, concerns, puzzles, complaints, frustrations, heart-melting joys, the amazing things you're learning. You all are there for each other. Take advantage of this!

### How to Lead an E-vent Group

Many of you are seasoned leaders and teachers. Some of you will be leading groups you have lead for years (youth, Sunday school classes, women's and men's groups, young adults' groups). Others are leading brand new groups, formed for this six-week season. Some of you may be leading a group for the first time. You will probably all learn something new. Here's the big thing:

> *Goal for Leaders:* **You are _not_ here to *TEACH*. You are here to help group members _experience_ the gospel, prayer and a loving Christian community. The less you talk, the better. The more group members talk about their thoughts, personal experiences of God and actually pray, the more they will get out of it! Pretend you're on a tandem bike. You just steer and help balance. Let the other one pedal.**

*A Word for Leaders of Large Ongoing Groups.* Since the goal is to help people talk about faith experiences that often feel very private, you may find that a short general discussion with the whole group works well. (See description below.) Then you may want to break into smaller groups of 8 to 10 to have more "cozy" discussions. Some groups choose to divide into smaller classes for the entire six weeks. This can give new leaders in your class a safe time to try their leadership wings in a nonthreatening way, with your support. You know your group. You decide, or ask them to choose!

When people have agreed to serve as leaders, please enter their names and contact information on the Small Group Leader Roster for New Groups *(Groups Form #23)*. A copy of these rosters goes to the E-vent Team as soon as possible.

*Leaders in Spiritual Agreement.* We have discovered a wonderful dynamic of leadership. Two people together lead better than one alone. While one is leading, the other can watch to see which kinds of leadership work best with your group. The nonleading leader should also be praying for the group and the co-leader. Talk about the week's session together ahead of time. Pray for your group members together at least once a week. (This conversation and prayer can be on the phone, over lunch, or before or after the All Leaders' Weekly Meeting.) Pray for each member of your group and the people Christ can reach through them each day. Pray for each other and the other teachers each day of the study. You may be surprised at what this can do for you, your friends, the church and people you don't even know yet.

### Good Group Dynamics Rules

How do you lead a group? Here are a few suggestions:

*Pray daily for each group member.* Pray that everyone in the group will get exactly what God would love them to learn from this experience. Leaders amplify the effect of the group if they pray for all the unknown people God can reach through the group members and the church. A member of the Prayer Team will be praying for your group. Find out who it is, and keep in touch. Don't share confidential details, but let this person know how he or she can focus prayer for your leaders and for the group.

*One leader leads, one leader prays.* When you are not leading the session, pray for group members and the group.

*Participate fully in weekly group leaders' meetings.* You get the best of both worlds — you can help others by leading a group. That's a profound experience, and you're helping Christ develop and grow his church. You also have the backup, support and growth we can only get by learning, talking from our depths, and praying with our peers. The group leaders' meetings are *your* small group.

*Confidentiality.* Ask your group if they are willing to commit to rules of group confidentiality at the first meeting. If everyone is willing, it is best if all sign a confidentiality agreement (*Groups Form #24*). This agreement is reinforced by a marginal notation next to the discussion questions at the end of each chapter of **Unbinding Your Heart.**

*Agree on preparation, punctuality & attendance.* Groups function best if each member commits to reading the chapter assigned *before* the group meeting each week. During the first session, when

---

*Goal for Leaders:*
You are *not* here to *TEACH*. You are here to help group members *experience* the gospel, prayer and a loving Christian community. The less you talk, the better. The more group members talk about their thoughts, personal experiences of God and actually pray, the more they will get out of it! Pretend you're on a tandem bike. You just steer and help balance. Let the other one pedal.

you discuss confidentiality, ask that they each do their individual prayer exercises in Part III of *Unbinding Your Heart* each day. Raise the bar high for preparation, punctuality and attendance! If the group agrees on clear expectations at the beginning of your six weeks, your time together will be happier and more productive!

***Fish for answers! Don't tell them!*** It's much better to ask questions than to state truths. People remember 90% of what we say and only 10% of what we hear! Leaders — let's make the E-vent memorable for our small group members. Try to help people express their own developing thoughts and feelings. "What do you think about this?" tends to be more helpful to people than, "The author says…"

***Get personal, avoid abstract discussions!*** The more group time spent doing exercises, talking about personal reactions, and actually praying, the better.

**First Week Small Group Agreements**

- confidentiality
- preparation
- punctuality
- attendance

Spend the ***first 10 minutes of each session*** helping people talk about how their individual prayer has gone this week. (This is listed as the first discussion question at the end of each chapter.)

***Length of Sessions.*** You have free scope here. Some groups love 50-minute or hour-long sessions. There is plenty of material for a two-hour discussion/experience. You might have normal sessions of one hour, but decide together to do a 4-hour "mini-retreat" one week. Feel free to create, but be in agreement as a leadership group. Make sure your specific group is also in agreement, in advance.

***Be punctual.*** Start and end on the minute of the appointed time. Group meetings that drag on and on are one of the major reasons for dissatisfaction with a new group. Keep time on discussion segments suggested for exercises precisely and signal ending times with a gong or bell. Honor the ending time. No matter how fabulous the discussion is at 7:59, end. On time!

***What to do each group session.*** The questions, exercises, and discussions of your individual prayer time are immensely flexible. Some groups would love to work with the scripture questions all hour. Others may tend to talk about their individual prayer for half the time. Others will be drawn to the discussion questions. Some will gravitate to the exercises. Let them do what they love, but try to make it as experiential as possible! If you're talking, don't let the discussion get too abstract. Try to ask questions about people's own experiences, feelings and life situations. Keep the focus on real life! Pray seriously each week.

***Do the exercises.*** We have discovered that groups that spend about half of their time praying and doing the experiential exercises over the course of the six-week study get the most out of it. Most people will want to do **anything but** the exercises. Push them a little! It's your job and it will help!

*Timing with Worship*. Sermons, music and worship liturgies will be coordinated with the study each week, if your pastor and worship team choose. Your church's members will get the most out of this coordination if they have read the chapter, met together and done the individual prayer exercises for the week **before** worship on Sunday. Worship and the sermon should help tie it all together for everyone.

### *Unbinding the Gospel* Compared to *Unbinding Your Heart*

*Leaders' Preparation*. We recommend that you read all of **Unbinding Your Heart** before the group begins. If you have participated in Step 1, the **Unbinding the Gospel** study, this will be easy — the heart of the book is exactly the same. I have added 40 days of individual prayer exercises that people can do alone and discuss with a prayer partner or with their families. (See the next chapter on the E-vent with Youth & Children.) The chapters correlate this way:

### Compare *Unbinding the Gospel* with *Unbinding Your Heart*

| Unbinding the Gospel: Real Life Evangelism | Unbinding Your Heart: 40 Days of Prayer & Faith Sharing |
|---|---|
| Chapter 1 and Chapter 3, *Breaking the Curse & Statistics* | Introduction (E-vent week 1) |
| Chapter 2, *Why **Do** Evangelism?* | Chapter 1 (E-vent week 1) |
| Chapter 4, *Three Stories of Victory* | Chapter 2 (E-vent week 2) |
| Chapter 5, *Real Life* | Chapter 3 (E-vent week 3) |
| Chapter 6, *What New Members Want* | Chapter 4 (E-vent week 4) |
| Chapter 7, *How's Your Church Doing?* | Chapter 5 (E-vent week 5) |
| Chapter 9, (8, 10) *Smart Sailing* | Chapter 6 (E-vent week 6) |
| | *40 Days of Prayer exercises start on Monday of Week One and continue throughout the six weeks of the E-vent* |

Read the introduction and the last chapter of **Unbinding Your Heart** before you begin leading your group. Converted chapters 2, 4, 5, 6, 7 and 9 from **Unbinding the Gospel** are shown with their new chapter numbers in **Unbinding Your Heart** in the table above. The end and the beginning of the book are edited. I have taken out

*Fish for answers! Don't tell them!* It's much better to ask questions than to state truths. We remember 90% of what we say and only 10% of what we hear! Leaders — let's make the E-vent memorable for our small group members. Try to help people express their own developing thoughts and feelings. "What do you think about this?" tends to be more helpful to people than, "The author says…"

quite a bit of material from chapters 1, 3, 8 and 10, but the existing chapters are almost exactly the same. The big addition is the 40 days of prayer. I hope you love them!

Please try to work through at least a week of the prayer exercises before your group sessions start. That way, you'll know the feel of them. Then you can decide to do the prayer days for the first time "with" your groups.

## All-Leaders' Weekly Meetings

Your E-vent will go smoothly if all leaders of E-vent small groups and the teachers/leaders of permanent classes in the church meet weekly to pray together and to compare notes. It may be easiest to get together for a common meal (if many of your groups meet at the same time in the same place), or before or after worship.

The Small Group Coordinator or someone well trained in teaching or group leadership skills can facilitate these meetings. Co-leadership of these meetings is great! You choose who would work best together for your people. You may want to invite a member of the Prayer Team to sit in your meetings and pray for you, them, and all the group members. You may not!

Group dynamics improve if you split a large group (over 14, not counting you as leaders) into smaller groups. This weekly Leaders' Meeting is your leaders' own small group. A smaller size fosters closeness and trust. A small group increases the participants' ability to share. If you all meet at the same time, you might meet together for a short time to deal with general issues, then split into smaller groups.

Here are my suggestions for your weekly meeting time. Use what's helpful to you:

- Remind everyone of your confidentiality agreements. They pertain to your leaders' meetings, too.
- Pray for each other, in groups of three, for the first ten minutes. Use the prayer exercise in chapter 11. *(Prayer Form #36)*
- Discuss how your groups are going. What's working well? What needs to be shifted? How are your members responding to the study? What are your biggest questions or frustrations? What exciting things are happening in your group? How's your prayer for your group going? How are group members changing?
- Look at next week's material, worship and events connected with the study. Plan and coordinate details (for example, the

prayer wall [week 1 for the children and week 2 for the rest of the church], the blessing of the church rooms [week 3], the prayer vigil and your celebration after the E-vent).

■ Pray together for each other, your group members, all the people they can help move into a deeper relationship with Christ or with the church, and for the church itself.

Have a wonderful time leading your group! I have discovered many life-long mainline church members, even pastors, who are quite shy about their faith. We don't wear our hearts on our sleeves! Just keep praying and gently urging people to talk openly, share and pray bravely! Wonderful things can unfold. When you're not sure what to do with your group, sit quietly for a moment and pray for everyone. Pray that Christ will speak into your mind any words that would be helpful to say. Be patient. God will work miracles if we are patient, pray and stay as open as we can be to the Spirit's nudges.

Many teachers are "doers." Here's a little gift for you. Can you let yourself to accept it?

---

### PERMISSION SLIP

This permission slip gives you _____

_____*(write your name here)* permission to be a little lazy one day. You may *not* do something. You can let something slide. (Laundry? Cutting the grass? Changing the oil? Doing something for the church?) Take an hour off, skip something *so long as you are using the time to pray, to praise God, and to learn how much God loves you!*

Blessings,

*Martha Grace Reese*          _____

Pastor's Signature

---

## Small Group Team Forms

(See page 82 for downloading instructions)

- Small Group Team Member Roster *(Groups Form #20)*
- Small Group Team Meeting Schedule *(Groups Form #21)*
- Small Group Member & Leader Roster, Existing Groups *(Groups Form #22)*
- Small Group Leader Roster, New Groups *(Groups Form #23)*
- Confidentiality Agreement *(Groups Form #24)*
- Small Group Team Weekly Checklist *(Groups Form #25)*
- Sign-up forms and small group rosters are listed with the E-vent Team Forms *(E-vent Forms #12–14)*

# The Prayer Team

### Who Prays During the E-vent?

Prayer is a crucial component of faith and of evangelism. You know this, if you have read **Unbinding the Gospel**. Prayer will be an essential element to your all-church study of **Unbinding Your Heart**. Think of all the ways that your church will be praying during the E-vent, not even counting what you will do as a Prayer Team:

- Your pastor and the whole church staff will pray daily for group leaders, church members, the church itself, and the people you can reach
- Small group leaders will pray daily
- Small group leaders will pray during their weekly meetings
- Each small group participant will covenant to use the 40 daily prayer exercises in **Unbinding Your Heart**

That's a substantial amount of prayer! Now we're asking you to ramp it up another notch! Will you form a Prayer Team that will start meeting weekly at least a month before the E-vent? Will you discern one person who participated in the Step 1 study of *Unbinding the Gospel* as a *Prayer Coordinator* for the E-vent? The qualities to look for are someone who

- prays consistently,
- is good with people and
- who likes to plan and organize!

## What Does the Prayer Team Do?

*All churches, large and small, need a Prayer Team*. Your Prayer Coordinator and your Prayer Team have three important jobs. First, Prayer Team members will pray for the church and the E-vent daily. They will also pray together once a week. Second, they will support and pray for the church's leadership. Third, they will organize prayer projects that the whole church can join in.

*Who should be part of the Prayer Team?* Think of the people who pray seriously. Some churches talk about "intercessors." Others speak of "prayer warriors." If your church has done a spiritual gifts study, who scored highest on gifts of wisdom, prayer and intercession? They're your natural Prayer Team candidates.

Do you have a prayer group? Can you think of junior or senior high school kids who are falling in love with Christ and would like to learn to pray better? Might your neighbor commit to join your team with you? (That would be the neighbor who loves to pray, used to be an elder in another church 12 years ago, but felt shredded by a church fight.) Do you know spiritual giants who are now shut-ins because of frail physical health? *These* are the people to ask to be part of your Prayer Team. Who says you have meet at the church?

Ask God who should be on the Prayer Team. Pray about it. Then ask them!

## 1. How to Pray Together as a Team

*Prayer Team*: Will you covenant to meet together once a week to pray for the E-vent, your church, its leaders and the people your church members can reach with the gospel? Discuss confidentiality at your first meeting *(Groups Form #24)*. Begin to pray together at least a month before the E-vent starts.

*Prayer Team's Weekly Meeting*. Structure your time together in a way that feels most comfortable to you and to your style of praying. Here is a suggestion. Modify it to fit your team members:

*Light a candle* to remind yourselves that Jesus is right there with you.

---

*The Prayer Team has three jobs:*

1. pray for the church,

2. support the church's leaders with prayer and

3. organize prayer events that the whole church can join in.

***Share how your individual prayer is going***. You can start the prayer exercises in ***Unbinding Your Heart*** as soon as you begin to meet. Use Question 1 at the end of each chapter for this discussion. (10 min.)

***Pray for each other in small groups of three*** *(Prayer Form #36)* (10 min.)

***Sit in silence***. Sit comfortably, with your spine straight and both feet on the floor. The prayer leader can begin the silence with a short prayer such as, "Lord Jesus, thank you for your love for us. Help us to relax and know you're really here. For just five minutes, we won't talk. We'll sit here and listen to you quietly." At the end of the silent prayer time, the Prayer Coordinator can say, "Amen," or ring a bell, or gently strike a gong — anything to signal that the silence is drawing to a close. (You will have random thoughts. They're normal. Just gently deflect them, like a little stick floating on the surface of a stream. And turn your attention back to God.) (5 min.)

***Gently say the Lord's Prayer together***. (Your leader will start the prayer.)

***Discuss how the E-vent is going***. What are you seeing? Go over what the Prayer Coordinator has learned from the Leadership Team. Prayer Coordinator — you could make a written list of things Prayer Team members can pray for during the coming week. Be sure *not* to put anything in writing that is confidential or sensitive. If you have any doubts, don't use names or share details that could betray a confidential situation. God knows who the prayer is for!

Pray together out loud for the things you have talked about and anything else the Spirit prompts you to pray for. Don't pray in flowery paragraphs! Single words and phrases are much better. Then everyone can concentrate on the situation or person named for five or ten seconds in silence. (*E.g.*, "Betty [our pastor]"…five second pause as everyone prays…"courage for the youth group as they invite their friends to the pizza party on Saturday"…five second pause as everyone prays…"melt our hearts for people who don't know God"…pause…). When the Prayer Coordinator senses that the prayer is done, s/he can offer a short close to the prayer, such as, "God, we thank you and praise you. In Jesus' name we pray. Amen."

Discuss how you will each be praying for the E-vent and the church until you meet again next week. Talk about any new ways you might like to pray together when you meet next.

Discuss any details about the organization of the congregation's prayer efforts. Your team will be responsible to organize any special prayer efforts you chose to try. (*See "Organize Prayer Activities for the*

Will you covenant to meet together once a week to pray for the E-vent, your church, its leaders and the people your church members can reach with the gospel? Discuss confidentiality at your first meeting. Begin to pray together at least a month before the E-vent starts.

*Whole Church"* on page 67.) Will you choose to construct a prayer wall? Hold a prayer vigil? Will you decide to be available to pray for individuals who come forward to the chancel area at the end of each worship service? How will you support the team leaders and members as they study and pray through the six-week E-vent?

### 2. Pray for & Encourage Your Church's Leaders

In addition to your weekly Prayer Team meetings, you might consider being intercessors for different individuals and groups of people who are serving as E-vent leaders. Here are a few ideas. You may choose to do a few of these. You may think of others. Ask God which to do.

*A. Encourage others to pray. Stay in touch.* The Prayer Team can pray for and encourage each of the types of prayer that will be going on during the E-vent. It might be helpful for the Prayer Coordinator to remind the pastors, the musicians, the E-vent Coordinator and small group leaders that you are praying for them in a short, encouraging e-mail each week. One of you might write little cards or notes. Thank them for their commitment to pray daily for the members of the groups they are leading. (A thank you is also a very polite reminder!) Different Prayer Team members could take turns doing this each week. Ask the leaders to let you know if there are specific ways you can be praying for them and for their groups.

*B. E-vent Leadership weekly meetings.* The Prayer Team Coordinator will be part of the E-vent Leadership weekly meetings. One of his/her ways of serving is to lead the 10 minutes of prayer for the team at the beginning of the meeting *(Prayer Form #36)*. The Prayer Team Coordinator can also pray for participants and the church during the meeting, then give the Prayer Team an update on how they can pray for the E-vent Leadership Team.

*C. Small Group Leaders' meetings; youth and children's leaders.* Could someone on the Prayer Team attend the Small Group Leaders' and the youth and children's weekly meeting? One of you may be leading a small group or working with the youth. If so, pray for the leaders through their meeting. (You could also share this prayer with people attending the meeting. What if you each took 5 minutes to pray for the meeting while it is going on? Open your eyes, see what's happening, but during all of your five minutes, pray for everyone there and the discussion that's going on. Pass someone's wristwatch around the circle. Hand it to the next person at the end of your five minutes to let the next person know it's "their watch!" If

---

**Intercessors' Confidentiality:**
Don't use names or identifying characteristics if you share a request for prayer that might be confidential or sensitive. You can ask the Prayer Team to help, but describe the situation as a category, without details (e.g., "a person who just found out their spouse is having an affair.") You could be as circumspect as, "Please pray for the situation I'm thinking about now."

you are divided up into little groups to discuss or pray, let the leader take over the intercession.)

*D. Prayer for everyone in the church.* You may choose to divide the congregation members among yourselves and pray for each of them every day. You may ask the deacons or the elders or a special Sunday school class to do this.

*E. Prayer for situations.* Which people, or what aspects of the E-vent need specific prayer? Are you running short of books? Do any group leaders feel awkward or out of their depth? Have any little personality glitches raised their ugly heads? Is the staff tired? Your job is to pray about it and to bring these situations back to the rest of the Prayer Team. Ask your pastor, or the person leading the Leaders' meeting to let you know what you can pray for specifically.

### Three rather random thoughts:

We have included a *weekly intercessor's prayer request list,* if that would be helpful to you as you pray for many people. (See *Prayer Form #33.*)

*Intercessors' Confidentiality:* Don't use names or identifying characteristics if you share a request for prayer that might be confidential or sensitive. You can ask the Prayer Team to help, but describe the situation as a category, without details (e.g., "a person who just found out their spouse is having an affair.") You could be as circumspect as, "Please pray for the situation I'm thinking about now."

*Please don't overburden yourself with lists and tasks.* Ask God which things you should be doing, which prayers you should be praying.

### 3. Organize Prayer Activities for the Whole Church

*The Prayer Team has three jobs: (1) pray for the church, (2) support the church's leaders with prayer and (3) organize prayer events that the whole church can join in.*

Here are suggestions for all-church prayer. Don't try to do all of them, especially if you're in a small congregation! We need to learn that prayer is not about killing ourselves with overwork. Prayer is opening ourselves to God. Prayer is helping our dear church members learn that God loves them. Over-functioning won't help that happen! But if we stop some of the busy-ness for just six weeks and really pray, the things that matter to God may begin to emerge.

Do you want to organize some of these possibilities for your church's E-vent?

**Please don't overburden yourself with lists and tasks.** Ask God which things you should be doing, which prayers you should be praying.

*Shut-ins* could each take names of people in the congregation (elders, deacons, the youth group) to pray for daily.

*Praying for each other at the beginning of every church meeting.* Would you agree, just for six weeks, to try an experiment? Will you start all of your E-vent meetings by praying for each other for 10 minutes using the same prayer style the other teams are using *(Prayer Form #36)? My* prayer is that this will become a habit for you and that you'll continue it for a year after the E-vent in every single meeting in your church.

*Prayer Requests.* Members will be able to place prayer requests in the offering plates each week of the E-vent. (See *Prayer Form #32.*)

*Prayer Wall.* Create a prayer wall outside the sanctuary. Stock a nearby table with pens, pencils and large, multicolored Post-It™ notes so that everyone can keep adding to the wall. Use the wall for prayer requests, notes of gratitude for answered prayers and reflections people would like to share. You might have one section of the wall made out of cork, with pushpins, so that people can post longer letters written at home. (The children will make the "stones" for the wall; the youth can "assemble" it. Offer support to the youth leaders. Prayer Coordinator — please see the full description of the prayer wall at the end of chapter 6. Copy this section for your team, if you think it would help them.)

*Prayer Vigil.* You might hold a prayer vigil at some point during the study. Tailor the time to fit your church. You could choose a short, six-hour vigil. You might arrange a 24-hour vigil. Let the Prayer Team (in conjunction with the E-vent Leadership Team) work out the timing and duration of the prayer vigil. You might want to have it at the beginning of the E-vent, or during the 24 hours leading up to the celebration to which you invite visitors at the end of the E-vent. Some congregations might want to have two prayer vigils — a short one by the Step 1 participants just before the E-vent begins, then a 24-hour vigil for the whole congregation at the end. Large congregations may want to have many people praying together during each half-hour segment. Adjust details to serve your congregation. (See two vigil sign-up sheet forms, *Prayer Forms #34 & 35.*)

*A Fast.* Your team could choose to fast, or you might ask if others will join you for a special day of holding back from something you normally do. Offer that little sacrifice to God (all food, using the Internet, meat, TV, alcohol, etc.)

*Prayer Activities You Could Organize:*

1. Shut-ins praying
2. 10 minutes of prayer at start of all church meetings
3. Prayer requests
4. Prayer wall
5. Prayer vigil
6. A fast
7. Prayer by children
8. Prayer coach, spiritual director
9. Intercession after worship

***Children's Sunday School***. Encourage teachers of each of the children's Sunday school classes to adapt one of the days of that week's prayer exercises for the children each week. Ask them if they have any specific prayer requests from their classes. Ask if there is any way you could focus your prayer for them, specifically.

***Prayer Coach? Spiritual Director?*** You may choose to ask someone who has prayed for years — an elder, a trained spiritual director — to be available to talk with people about their prayer experiences after your worship service. Could you arrange for a spiritual director to talk with your prayer group and with the small group leaders at one of your first meetings? The more encouragement and back-up your leaders have, the better!

***Prayer for Individuals after Worship***. Ask intercessors from the Prayer Team to pray individually for people who come forward to the front of the sanctuary after the worship service. Listen to each person's prayer request carefully. Don't talk much, but hear what they're saying carefully. You might put one hand on their shoulder as you pray for them.

## A Final Word for the Prayer Team

Don't do too much. Spread out the load. Ask others to help you with prayer. The more we can support others' praying, the more they will learn to love to connect with God in prayer. Love the Lord, teach prayer, enjoy every moment of this! Close your eyes and see if your jaw is tight. Is your brow furrowed? If the answer is yes, slow down, sit, pray and ask for help. May this time be a joyous adventure. Blessings upon each of you.

We need to learn that prayer is not about killing ourselves with overwork. Prayer is opening ourselves to God. Prayer is helping our dear church members learn that God loves them. Over-functioning won't help that happen! But if we stop some of the busy-ness for just six weeks and really pray, the things that matter to God may begin to emerge.

---

## PERMISSION SLIP

This permission slip gives you _____

(*write your name here*) permission to be lazy one day. ***Don't*** do

something. Let something slide. (Laundry? Cutting the grass?

Changing the oil? Organizing an E-vent prayer activity? Doing

something for church?) Take an hour off and drink a cup of

tea as you stare out a window. Skip something *so long as you*

*are using the time to pray, to praise God, and to learn how*

*much God loves you!*

Blessings,

*Martha Grace Reese*        _____

                                                Pastor's Signature

---

### Prayer Team Forms

(See page 82 for downloading instructions)

- Prayer Team Member Roster (*Prayer Form #30*)
- Prayer Team Meeting Schedule (*Prayer Form #31*)
- Prayer Request (*Prayer Form #32*)
- Intercessor's Weekly Prayer List (*Prayer Form #33*)
- Prayer Vigil (Noon Start) (*Prayer Form #34*)
- Prayer Vigil (Midnight Start) (*Prayer Form #35*)
- Prayer Exercise for the Beginning of All Team Meetings (*Prayer Form #36*)
- Prayer Team Weekly Checklist (*Prayer Form #37*)

# CHAPTER SIX

# Children and Youth

### Highlights of Chapter 6

- The E-vent Is for Kids too!
- New Research on Youth and Faith Development
- Youth Study of Unbinding Your Heart
- The E-vent with Families
- Youth Leaders — Your Youths' E-vent Group
- Prayer, the Most Important Ingredient
- A Few Final Thoughts

### The E-vent Is for Kids too!

The E-vent is for kids, too. We hope that every youth from middle school and older will participate in an E-vent small group. Middle school and senior high groups can do E-vent groups just as the adults do. If your confirmation class is meeting during the E-vent, we suggest that you use *Unbinding Your Heart* and its prayer exercises as your curriculum.

We suggest that teachers of younger children's Sunday school or after-school classes incorporate one of the prayer exercises or an age-adapted exercise from the end of the week's chapter in each week's lesson. This will help the younger kids be part of the on-going congregational excitement over the E-vent.

In churches that have had an E-vent, some families have decided to do their daily prayer exercises at the same time. Some middle school kids set up a little altar on the coffee table. Other children, without prompting, made a worship centerpiece on the family dinner table while their family was doing the prayer exercises. (It had candles and a rosary that had belonged to a great aunt.) Another family (a mother with one daughter) decided not to eat on the couch in front of the TV a couple of times a week. They set the table and talked about what had happened that week in their prayer times.

These examples were a surprise. Some came from families in which one parent was "testing" the prayer exercises for me. I had not asked them to mention the prayers to the family. I had never thought of kids getting involved with these prayer exercises. The kids — grade school, middle school, and senior high school students — read the prayers and started doing them. After a bit more testing, I am clear that children and youth can participate in the E-vent in the following ways:

*That* is the purpose of the E-vent — to help us realize that if our faith lives, we have something important to share. If we aren't alive in Christ, it doesn't matter much whether we do evangelism or not. We're trying to help people enter into a relationship with God of their *own*. Let's start with ourselves and with our kids.

- doing 40 days of prayer
- in worship
- in their youth groups or Sunday school classes
- and with their families

### New Research on Youth and Faith Development

A huge, new study of American young people raised their whole lives in the church has found that most of our kids have a hard time articulating the most basic tenets of the faith. They have a hard time talking about their personal faith. The researchers discovered that this difficulty exists as much among youth raised in very conservative congregations (with great emphasis on Bible study and testimonies) as with kids from the most theologically liberal churches! If you ask most religiously raised young people what it means to be a Christian, the typical answer is that being Christian has to do with being a good person and doing good things for people.[1]

Strangely enough, this is almost exactly what we discovered in the Mainline Evangelism Project. We asked hundreds of mainline **pastors** what difference it made in their own lives that they were Christian. The most frequent first response was, "Because it makes me a better person"???[2]

We can do better than this! We can connect vividly with Christ, with God, with the Spirit in prayer, in worship and as we go about our everyday lives. *That* is the purpose of the E-vent — to help us realize that if our faith lives, we have something important to share. If we aren't alive in Christ, it doesn't matter much whether we do evangelism or not.

The point of evangelism is to share the exciting relationship we are living with God with people who don't know God. We're trying to help people enter into a relationship with God of their *own*. Let's start with ourselves and with our kids.

How do we start to teach our children and youth about the core of the faith? The researchers discovered that, in addition to a great Christian community with the mission trips and fun kids need and love, kids need two main things to grow into healthy, solid Christian adults:

1. solid, adult role models with whom they can talk about God, their lives, their developing faith

2. real spiritual lives, grounded in classic Christian prayer practices

Does this sound familiar? It's what we are trying to do with adults in the E-vent! The two main things we adults need are to strengthen our prayer and faith lives, and to learn to talk about them. We pastors need to learn it. We adults need to learn it. We teachers need to learn it. All of our kids need to learn it! It's time. Let's have a faith life. Let's talk about our faith life. We can do this!

*A suggestion for your youth team (and parents).* If you'd like to go even further than the E-vent with your youth and with your own spiritual life, please read Mark Yaconelli's *Contemplative Youth Ministry: Practicing the Presence of Jesus*[3] prior to your E-vent if you can. If you can't get to it in time, please put it first on your post–E-vent reading list! It isn't geared to religious sociologists and seminary faculty. It is a down-to-earth, practical book on how to work with teenagers, based on solid research. After you read it, I suspect you'll want to try Yaconelli's approach with the kids with whom God has entrusted *you*.

Children and youth can participate in the E-vent in the following ways:

- doing 40 days of prayer
- in worship
- in their youth groups or Sunday school classes
- with their families

## Youth Study of *Unbinding Your Heart*

We recommend that all junior and senior high youth do the E-vent in their youth groups. Senior high youth can read the book easily. Most junior high classes will be able to read and discuss the book. You may need to do short presentations of chapter contents for some of the chapters, depending on your group. Skip the introduction with most kids, and go straight to chapter 1. (On the other hand, you may want to read them the beginning of the Introduction and show them a film clip of the end of the 2004 World Series, when the Boston Red Sox broke "The Curse.") *The important point is for your youth to work with the prayer exercises every day, to have a short discussion of the chapter, and to do the exercises at the ends of the chapters together.*

*Make sure all the kids have Bibles of their own <u>before</u> the E-vent starts.* Make sure they know how to look up the scriptures each day for the prayer exercises. It may be a good idea to have them look up the scriptures for the upcoming week during group time. They can help each other and write down the page numbers for their Bibles on the right pages of this week's prayers in *Unbinding Your Heart.*

Younger children could at least do **one** *Unbinding Your Heart* prayer exercise each week during their Sunday school or study time. It would be best to coordinate the children's weekly exercise so that the younger children are ahead of everyone else, rather than being left behind. That will be cool for them!

### The E-vent with Families

*The Goal:* to help each person in the congregation (a) experience a living connection with God, and (b) begin to talk about their faith. *The Means to the Goal:* the E-vent.

One of the most natural places for youth to talk about their faith is in their families, but, unfortunately, it doesn't happen in most families. Parents often fear doing something wrong or not **knowing** enough to talk with kids about the values they need to talk about when they're growing up. Adults (and parents) back quietly toward the door when they think about talking with kids about scary topics such as drugs, sex or their faith! Many parents clam up. They unconsciously rely on schools and churches to give their kids an ethical and faith foundation.

*The Family E-vent — Start with a parents' meeting.* You can help God bless the youth and the families in your church if you'll have a meeting several weeks *before* the E-vent to talk about family participation in the E-vent. *Ask the parents* if they will be willing to participate faithfully in an E-vent study group **and** do the 40 days of prayer exercises at the back of *Unbinding Your Heart.* Then ask if they will *talk* about what each of them is learning or experiencing with the rest of their family members.

If the parents agree, they might want to have one family dinner a week, at the table, talking together. Each member of the family could talk about two things:

1. This is what happened when I prayed this week...
2. I saw God today when...

During your parents' meeting, ask the parents if this feels scary to them! Let them talk about that. See if you can help them move to a

The two main things we adults need are to strengthen our prayer and faith lives, and learn to talk about them. We pastors need to learn it. We adults need to learn it. We teachers need to learn it. All of our kids need to learn it! It's time. Let's have a faith life. Let's talk about our faith life. We can do this!

place where they're willing to commit to a test of themselves praying each day and talking about their faith if their kids will agree to do it, too. It's only six weeks. The parents will have their own adult group in which to work on these ideas and to start to learn to articulate their own faith. They can practice with their friends, **then** try to talk with their kids. That may be **way** less threatening!

You might designate a team member to keep in touch with the parents during the E-vent to see if they're doing all right, have any questions, or need specific prayer. How about one parents' "check-in" over coffee a couple of weeks into the E-vent? How about another meeting after the E-vent? What worked well? What was challenging? Would the families like to keep going in this direction?

### Youth Leaders — Your Youths' E-vent Group

How do you lead your youth's E-vent group? Try to help them experience the wonder of God in prayer, then help them talk about it. Be real yourself. Try the exercises at the end of each chapter of **Unbinding Your Heart** with your youth. Most of them shouldn't be too complicated or abstract. Tailor them to your kids if you need to. Be sure to ask them to talk about how their individual prayer is going. Pray together each meeting.

Other ways to help children and youth talk about their faith is to ask, "where have you seen God today?" Perhaps you could ask them to take a silent, solitary walk around the church for 10 or 15 minutes. Ask them not to talk at all, but instead to look and listen, to pay attention to whatever is there. (Okay, they can talk if someone not in the group says hi to them, or needs directions — this doesn't need to get weird or rude!)

When they return, ask them what they saw. Were there bugs under leaves? What did they hear? Did they have any feelings that were different than when they're walking around listening to their iPods™ or talking to their friends? Discuss what they experienced. Do they see God in anything that happened on their walk?

We all need to slow down and see what's right in front of our noses. If we do this, after a while, we'll have a much better chance to see what's really there. We'll have a better chance of knowing ourselves. We may discover some buried emotions that are driving us. We might glimpse God creating something new. We could meet Jesus, feel the promptings of the Spirit, recognize answered prayer. If we slow down, life gets more **real**.

> The important point is for your youth to work with the prayer exercises every day, to have a short discussion of the chapter, and to do the exercises at the ends of the chapters together.

## Prayer, the Most Important Ingredient

*Pray for the youth you serve*. Will you pray for each of your youth and children every day?

*Prayer Partners*. Ask the youth if they will work with a prayer partner during the week to talk about how their individual prayers are going. If they would like to try prayer partners, be careful about how they are selected. Young people who are new, or feel socially on the fringes of the group could feel uncomfortable. Avoid the dynamic of anyone feeling like the last fourth grader picked for the dodge ball team! You leaders may need to take a hand in the selection process.

*Make sure all the kids have Bibles of their own <u>before</u> the E-vent starts.* Make sure they know how to look up the scriptures each day for the prayer exercises. It may be a good idea to have them look up the scriptures for the upcoming week during group time.

If you choose to do prayer partners, they could meet in person, online, or on the phone. Let them talk a couple of times a week about how their daily prayer is going. See if one of the Prayer Team members will be willing to pray for the youth in your class and their families each day of the E-vent. If all youth have easy access to computers, you may want to set up the prayer partnering on the church's Web site or suggest that the kids use instant messaging to talk about their prayers as well as talking on the phone or in person.

*Prayer "Sponsors."* The elders or adult sponsors might be willing to work with the teens one-on-one as prayer partners during the E-vent. (Do you do sponsors for your confirmation youth? This can be a great model!) Our kids need solid adults who will listen to them, who will occasionally share stuff they're really thinking.

*Prayer for the E-vent with Your Children and Youth*. Reread the second story in chapter 2 of **Unbinding Your Heart**. Do you remember the story of the Prayer Walkers during vacation Bible school? Is there a way you can fit that into your ministry with your kids and youth? It would be wonderful for everyone. Stay in touch with the members of the Prayer Team who will be praying for the kids specifically. Invite them to your team meetings and to the parents' meetings. They will help undergird all of your work with prayer.

*Kids Build the Prayer Wall.* You could build a prayer wall on a large space of common area in the church. Get pictures of the Wailing Wall in Jerusalem from a book or from the Internet. The Wailing Wall is the only remaining wall of the second temple. The Roman army destroyed the rest of the temple in 70 A.D. ("A.D." stands for "*__Anno__ __Domini__*" or "the year of our Lord." Some people use C.E. instead, meaning the "__Common Era__.") This is one of the most holy places in Jerusalem. Jews from all over the world go there to pray.

During the *first week of the E-vent,* bring paper grocery bags for each of the children in your Sunday school classes. Help them cut out large brown "stones" from the two big sides of each bag.

Some children might want to make big triangles, others round stones, others rectangular. Help them draw three or four stones from each paper bag. Let the children ask God to help them "name" their stones for people they know. Pray, "Lord Jesus, please show me a person to pray for, who will be part of our prayer wall." When they know who each stone stands for, write the first name of the person ("Buddy" or "Grandma Ann") on the back of the stone. Stand in a circle, with the children holding their stones. Pray for the people.

Encourage the children to say the names out loud during the prayer.

*Then let the older kids (in the junior high and/or high school group) assemble the stones into a "wall," anchoring each brown stone with masking tape.* The older youth might want to make a huge, mosaic, construction paper cross to put in the middle or at the end of the wall. Let the wall be in place to greet worshipers before the second week of the E-vent. The sermon that week will help everyone in the congregation pray for a person the way the children did with the stones. The adults will write their names on Post-It™ notes. After worship, everyone will put their Post-It™ notes on the prayer wall.

*For the rest of the E-vent, people can add Post-It™ notes or rolled-up, tied-with-ribbon scrolls of paper to the wall.* Each note or scroll stands for an answered prayer or a prayer for a person or a situation. Ask everyone to use just first names or initials of people so that no one feels as if they are betraying a confidence.

Ask the children and youth in your Sunday school classes to identify prayer requests and answered prayers each week. Stop at the prayer wall with your classes and groups and encourage them to post new prayers, to read the names and to pray together in silence for everyone's prayers.

The Prayer Team will leave pens and pads of Post-It™ notes on a table by the prayer wall. Anyone can add a name. Anyone can pray by the wall throughout the E-vent.

*The Goal:* to help each person in the congregation (a) experience a living connection with God, and (b) begin to talk about their faith. The *Means to the Goal:* the E-vent.

## A Few Final Thoughts

*Web and Blogs.* Could someone set up an Internet site for the kids to talk about prayer, what they're learning about evangelism and what they're experiencing during the E-vent? We have discovered that Web discussion groups can *help* communication for both children and adults, but they are not as effective as face-to-face meetings. Use them for follow-up discussions. Don't try to replace person-to-person contact!

*YouTube and MySpace.* Where's your team of techies? Would you like to make a movie of your E-vent? How about a film crew to do interviews about how the prayer is changing people's lives? Think of the visuals: the prayer wall (with the little kids describing it in the second week of worship), candles at the vigil, the Easter Egg hunt, a talk with someone about what their faith means to them. This could be cool! Post it on YouTube and MySpace as well as your church Web site. Send it to me! I'll post the best ones on our Web site. (Contact us through *www.GraceNet.info*.) The rest of us can't wait to see what you do!

*E-vent Celebration with Children and Youth.* If your church is doing a final invite-your-friends celebration, be sure to plan children and youth components. Use your creativity and have the kids design their own invitations to their friends! Have a great time at the party!

*Relax!* Working with youth and children can be a 24/7 job. I'll bet a lot of you are parents of children and teenagers as well as doing all those dishes at home and working with kids at church. We parents tend to run ourselves ragged, not sleep enough and skimp on our own exercise and spiritual lives. Could you give yourself permission to slow down a little and let God do some more of the work? Will you stop doing all the duties once a week during the E-vent and pray instead? If you will, here's a permission slip to bag something important — even something in the church or for these great kids!

If the parents agree, they might want to have one family dinner a week, at the table, talking together. Each member of the family could talk about two things:

1. This is what happened when I prayed this week...

2. I saw God today when...

---

Download youth & children's curriculum at www.GraceNet.info. Go to Download Resources, then Exclusive Downloads, then enter the password: unbinding.

---

**PERMISSION SLIP**

This permission slip gives you _____

_____(write your name here) permission to be a little lazy one day. **_Don't_** do something. Let something slide. (Laundry? Cutting the grass? Changing the oil? Doing something for church? Do you do anything because you have to be perfect, rather than because it really matters? Don't do **_that_** thing!) Take an hour off and drink a cup of tea as you stare out a window. Skip something **_so long as you are using the time to pray, to praise God, and to learn how much God loves you!_**

Blessings,

_Martha Grace Reese_

_____
Pastor's Signature

Pray, "Lord Jesus, please show me a person to pray for, who will be part of our prayer wall." When they know who each stone stands for, write the first name of the person ("Buddy" or "Grandma Ann") on the back of the stone. Stand in a circle, with the children holding their stones. Pray for the people.

---

[1]Mark Yaconelli, *Contemplative Youth Ministry: Practicing the Presence of Jesus* (Grand Rapids, Mich.: Zondervan/Youth Specialties, 2006).

[2]See Martha Grace Reese, *Unbinding Your Heart* (St. Louis: Chalice Press, 2008), chap. 1.

[3]Yaconelli, *Contemplative Youth Ministry.*

# CHAPTER 7

# Evaluation

## *What Have You Learned? What's Next?*

Don't let the great ideas and spiritual excitement of the E-vent evaporate. Evaluate!

At the end of the E-vent, ask each group to summarize what they have learned. Please tell what's happened and make suggestions for the church *in writing*. Gather the E-vent leadership a month or so after the end of the E-vent. Think through the written statements. Discuss the church's experience during the E-vent and what you have learned. Your leadership could go on a retreat to help you think through what you have learned.

Report your suggestions and findings to the church leadership — the elders, the council, the Evangelism Team. How will you create structures to "institutionalize" the creativity? What are the three most important steps you can take to help the church continue the E-vent's momentum?

### Unbinding Your Future

1. See www.GraceNet.info for my suggested "mini-retreat" plan, the "Unbinding Your Future Retreat."

2. I would like to leave you with an ongoing suggestion. Would you be willing to begin every meeting, every small group in your church with the 10-minute prayer exercise we've been doing at the beginnings of meetings (*Prayer Form 36*)? Will each group pray in groups of three at the beginning of each meeting — the

church board, deacons, elders, women's and men's groups, the choir, the crew of die-hards who meet to mow the grass and clean out the gutters?) Will you try it for six months? Then reevaluate. Decide whether God is calling you to continue doing it for the next six months! See what God can do with that tithe of meeting time!

3. *Unbinding Your Soul.* Don't slip back to normal! We are discovering that the "high" of the E-vent can dissipate and become a wonderful memory if we don't provide structures that continue our new habits: prayer, real talk, invitation. *Unbinding Your Soul* is your next step. It's simple — just small group curriculum to help people invite their friends to try an "experiment in prayer and community." *Soul* isn't the big E-vent — it's small group curriculum to help the momentum of the E-vent ("pre-evangelism") move into actual evangelism. *Soul* is where most churches are seeing significant numerical growth.

Blessings on you. Blessings upon your ministry. Thank you for giving your lives to God. It matters! MGR

---

Download free sermons, organizational forms, youth & children's curriculum and our "next steps" planning model (the Unbinding Your Future Retreat) at www.GraceNet.info. Go to Download Resources, then Exclusive Downloads, then enter the password: unbinding.

# Unbinding Your Church

# PART TWO

## Worship and Organization

■ **PART ONE** explores why and how to help your church start doing evangelism. How do you plan an all-church study of faith, prayer and faith sharing that could get some momentum going? What is the best timing, pacing, style of leadership for small groups? prayer groups? How do you organize to help your people change their habits, not just their minds?

■ **PART TWO** gives you integrated worship plans for your all-congregational experience of prayer and faith, your "E-vent!" Get sermons, music designs by four very different musicians, scriptures and prayers. Part II also provides you with forms, lists and organizational aids to help your church plan for and carry through an integrated, organized E-vent.

*Praise the Lord!*
*Praise God in his sanctuary;*
  *praise him in his mighty firmament!*
*Praise him for his mighty deeds;*
  *praise him according to his surpassing greatness!*

*Praise him with trumpet sound;*
  *praise him with lute and harp!*
*Praise him with tambourine and dance;*
  *praise him with strings and pipe!*
*Praise him with clanging cymbals;*
  *praise him with loud clashing cymbals!*
*Let everything that breathes praise the Lord!*
*Praise the Lord!*

*Psalm 150*

# CHAPTER 8

# The E-vent in Worship

## *Scriptures and Sermon Outlines*

### *by Dawn Darwin Weaks*

Dear colleagues,

I did my best to write these sermons and worship materials with you in mind — you, in your various settings of ministry and sizes of churches. I included personal stories from my ministry or from close colleagues' experiences. But I made them as general as possible for you to use in the ways that serve your congregation best. I included my convictions about the "E" word ("evangelism") but phrased it in Martha Grace Reese's language so we would be speaking the same lingo. You were on my mind and in my prayers every step of the way. I'm grateful to Joey Jeter for his insights into this work. I pray that something I've done will be useful to you and to Jesus.

But, when I came right down to it, I had to write for my own congregation. We'll be doing the "E-vent" here soon with my stuff. I can't wait to see what these committed Christian people do with it. You'll have to write, and preach, and pray for your own people, too, of course. Use the outlines, pluck out the illustrations, swap phrases from the prayers, preach a sermon verbatim — take whatever's helpful. Or, go off on your own completely. May what I've done be a diving board into the deep fountain of God's refreshment for you and your people.

Dawn

### A Note on Doing "Show and Tell":

Amy and Christian Piatt use this idea in their new church in Colorado. (They named it "show and tell.") Martha Grace Reese talks about it in chapter 6 of ***Unbinding the Gospel***. But the idea is as old as the Psalms. Psalm 145:4 says, "They will tell of your wonderful works to the next generation" (paraphrase). Getting people to stand up in worship and say how God has changed their lives is essential to helping others tune in to what God wants them to do. I'm guilty of only using testimonies for stewardship season. (You know, those three-minute treatises on "what this church means to me"?) In the last few years I've begun to ask people to talk about what God is doing in their lives on days other than stewardship Sunday. It is more effective than any sermon I've ever preached.

So, begin praying now about who in your congregation needs to stand up and tell of God's wonderful works. Ask God to get them ready for you to ask. Read through the descriptions of the "Show and Tell" for each Sunday. Who fits the bill? Let the Spirit lead you to people you wouldn't have thought of on your own. Be sure to give them plenty of notice. Coach them by asking them to tell you, in their own words, what they want to say. Help them say the essentials so they can be brief. Before Sunday morning, you or someone else needs to show them how to use the microphone, where to sit, and when to come up to speak. Standing up to speak before others, giving a testimony about deep and private things, can be nerve-wracking for the uninitiated. Be sure to help them prepare. Be sure to pray for them before, during, and after their experience.

Don't skip the "Show and Tell," whatever you do. Your people will hear these words best.

### Worship Outlines

Download full manuscripts for each sermon from www.GraceNet.info. Your password is on page 82.

---

---

**Sermon Title:** *The Baptism Barrier*

**Scripture:** Acts 8:26–37; Psalm 107:1–9

**Theme:** Are we creating barriers for people who need God's love?

**Note:** Use this sermon and worship service on Sign-up Sunday, six weeks before the E-vent. It's a "teaser" for what is to come. Commission your E-vent leadership by asking them to stand while you offer a special prayer for their work. You could ask them to come forward to be blessed.

**Symbol**: Hand out bottle "grips" (those thin, circular, rubber bottle openers) with your church logo on them to all worshipers, if you use the water bottle analogy.

**Scripture Sentences**: The book of Acts was written by Luke, the same person who wrote the Gospel, one of the stories of Jesus' life. Acts takes the next steps and tells us what the first Christians did next. How did they act after seeing Jesus risen from the dead? What did they do? Who did they tell about Jesus? Acts tells us about how the church grew. As the church got bigger, people who were not followers of Jesus felt threatened. They didn't trust this new twist on Judaism. Their mistrust grew into persecution. In chapter 7, Luke tells us about the first follower of Jesus who was killed because of his faith. His name was Stephen. In chapter 8, we hear this story about Stephen's friend, Philip. Philip is still bravely and boldly telling people about Jesus, even though Stephen had just been killed for his faith.

**Sermon Outline**

1. Have you ever thought of yourself as an evangelist?
     We have resistance to the word *evangelism*
     Reasons for our discomfort
          Stereotypes
          We don't know what to say
          Who am I to say anything?
2. But what happens when someone enters our lives who needs God?
     Ethiopian eunuch's story
     Rick's story (or a story about a completely unchurched person
          you've encountered)
     Statistics of the unchurched in your community

3. Are we the barrier that keeps people from God's love?

  Water bottle analogy (Hold up the "grip")

    Would you let someone struggle to open a bottle if you had a "grip"?

    That is what we do when we have the gospel but don't share it

  Philip seemed to have it easy

  Would it be like that for us?

4. Join the adventure of the *Unbinding Your Heart* study.

  Emily's story (or other illustration about the simplicity of helping someone)

  Philip sits down to guide the man

  Who are you sitting beside?

---

---

**Sermon Title**: *The Paul Problem*

**Scripture**: Isaiah 60:1–5a; Acts 9:1–19

**Theme**: Even though we may not have a dramatic conversion story to tell, we still have a lot to say about our faith!

**Symbol**: Set pitchers full of water in a display in the sanctuary or narthex. Or, using heavyweight fishing line, hang large pitchers from the ceiling in central places. Use a beautiful blue fabric to fill the pitchers to "overflow" out onto the floor below. You could even have the fabric extend across the altar of your worship space.

**Call to Worship**

> *Leader*: Lift up your hearts!
> *People:* **We lift them up to the Lord!**
> *Leader*: May God unbind our hearts.
> *People*: **May the love of Jesus Christ set our lives free.**
> *All*: **May the Spirit pour down upon us!**

**Show and Tell:** Look for someone who has been a Christian for a long time. You do not want someone who has a dramatic conversion story to tell. (Not yet! Save that person for the "Catalytic Conversations" sermon!) Look for someone who was raised in the church **and** seems to know why it's important. Consider: Which faithful member occasionally invites her friends to church, or makes sure her grandchildren attend? Or, which longtime Christian appreciates how God brought him through a tough life experience? Ask that person to sit down with you for a few minutes. Do this at least two weeks before the Sunday you want the testimony. Tell him or her you're hoping to help congregation members get more comfortable talking about their faith. Ask this person to pray and consider sharing in worship how being a Christian has made a difference. Then, a few days later, on the phone or in person, listen to what your "witness" plans to say. Give some coaching on being brief and joyful. Do a rehearsal in the sanctuary if you think it would help. Encourage and pray for him or her!

**Scripture Sentences**: Acts is a history book within the Bible. It tells us about the first Christians. What happened to them after Jesus ascended to heaven? They immediately faced people who wanted to run them out of town. Saul was one of the chasers! Saul was a very religious man. He thought he knew all he needed to know about God. He strongly disagreed with the new revelations about God brought by Jesus. He saw it as **his** godly mission to shut down the Christian mission. The ninth chapter of Acts tells us what happened when Saul met Jesus and a Christian named Ananias.

**Sermon Outline**

1. Do you need a dramatic conversion story to be able to talk about God?

    Jealous of people who have a dramatic tale to tell

    Paul's story made a clear difference in his life

    We don't all have a story like that

2. What difference does being a Christian make to you?

    Pastors' group illustration (or other story of a longtime Christian articulate about faith)

    Imagine your life without Christ

        What are the specific things you would miss?

        Again, what difference does being a Christian make?

    *[layperson's Show and Tell]*

3. What are your motivations for telling someone about Christ?

    Pitcher illustration showing being filled with motivations to share your faith

    Motivations named in the "Show and Tell

    What about Hell (or not Hell?)

4. Do you believe people are living in Hell on Earth?

    Saul's story of being in the dark for three days

    Sheena's story (or other story about reaching out to a truly despairing person)

5. What motivated Ananias to go tell Saul about Jesus?

    Jesus commanded him (is that enough?)

    He wanted to be a part of what God is doing in the world

    Where will God send you?

**Benediction:** May God guide our feet to obey; may God guide our mouths to speak; may God guide our hearts to love, in Jesus' name. Amen.

---

---

**Sermon Title:** *The Prayer Plunge*

**Scripture:** 1 Kings 19:11−13; Luke 5:1−10

**Theme:** Let's try an experiment in prayer and see what happens.

**Symbol:** Get your prayer wall up on the wall before worship. (See chapter 6.) Have large Post-It™ notes inside worship bulletin, pencils near seats to write prayers on adhesive notes. Each person will put the prayer on the prayer wall after worship.

**Call to Worship**

> *Leader:* Lift up your eyes!
> *People:* **From where does our help come?**
> *Leader:* Our help comes from the Lord, the Maker of Heaven and Earth!
> *People:* **Nothing comes from our effort alone.**
> *All:* **Only God brings fruit to our faithfulness!**

**Show and Tell:** Ask one of the youth who helped assemble the prayer wall to talk about the Wailing Wall in Jerusalem, and about how the youth assembled our wailing wall here. Ask one of the little children who made stones for the prayer wall to tell about making the "stones." Let him/her share who one particular stone is for and what it was like to pray for that person last Sunday, all standing in a circle and saying the names out loud to God. See chapter 6 for an explanation of how to integrate the children's stories and the prayer wall into the worship service.

**Scripture Sentences:** Luke is one of four books in the New Testament that tell the story of Jesus' life. These books were originally written in Greek. We call these stories of Jesus' life "Gospels," translating a Greek word that means "good news." The names of the gospels are: Matthew, Mark, Luke and John. Each of them tells us about Jesus choosing a very close group of friends to follow him. At one point in Luke's version, Jesus is preaching by a lake. The crowds keep growing, because word got out that Jesus heals people. Now there are so many people around Jesus that he doesn't have a place to stand. So he goes over to some of the fishermen by the shore and steps into one of their boats. It's Simon's boat. Jesus had just healed Simon's mother-in-law, so Simon knew Jesus and was certainly willing to help him out.

**Sermon Outline**

1. Are churches declining because we're lazy?

   NO! We work plenty hard!

   I'm inclined to give you more work to do, which must wear you out

   Maybe that's how the disciples felt when Jesus came to them

2. Jesus invites them back into the deep water with him.

   Deep water can be scary

   Scuba illustration (any story about how relaxing helped you do something well)

   Jesus wants them to understand something before they go to work with him

3. Prayer is one way that we can "go deep" with Jesus.

   Do we pray as much as we work? Could we?

   Benton Street's story (or another story about prayer going before the work)

   Going into the deep waters with Jesus makes a difference (Luke 5:6)

4. For the next month, let's pray like we've never prayed before.

   Prayer experiment in worship

   Prayer wall explanation

   Challenge to let "stuff" slide to set aside time for prayer

5. I believe God will do some amazing things with us during this time.

   Like the disciples, we may not be ready for what God wants to do

   But Jesus says, "Fear not"

   Will you go fishing in the deep water?

**Benediction:** May God guide our schedules to obey; may God guide our hearts to pray; may God guide our minds to believe, in Jesus' name. Amen.

---

---

**Sermon Title**: *The Converted Community*

**Scripture**: Acts 2:14, 32–39; Micah 6:6–8

**Theme**: Healthy relationships with other people in the church make a big difference in the effectiveness of our witness.

**Symbol**: Set up a place for people to wash each other's hands or feet by your prayer wall. Be sure you have a copy of the "Trinity of Relationships" drawing as a bulletin insert, and pencils for the congregation within easy reach.

**Call to Worship**

> *Leader:* Lift up your relationships!
> > Family, friends, neighbors, coworkers, brothers and sisters
> > > in Christ.
> > We place them in the light of God's love!
> *People:* **Let God's Spirit rule over every relationship.**
> *All*: **May we together live out the grace and peace of**
> > **Christ!**

**Show and Tell**: This is a sensitive assignment. Has God given anyone in your church a reconciled relationship? Might they be willing to tell about it in worship? Best of all would be for two people in the church to share their experience of being at odds and then forgiving one another. This type of a testimony would require great humility. Please do not force it. Meet with anyone who agrees to talk about such a time. Coach them on how to present it. They don't need to mention many details. Suggest they simply acknowledge that tensions existed, and then focus their testimony on how they allowed God to work things out between them, on what God did, and what happened.

Another option is to find someone who can share an experience of forgiveness in his or her life. Is there a person who could talk about the freedom that came when God forgave him or her? Be sure to pray for God's guidance for choosing your "witness" and for his or her sharing.

**Scripture Sentences**: In the first chapter of Acts, Jesus promised his disciples that he would send them the Holy Spirit to help them. After he ascended to Heaven, the disciples waited and prayed together for days. Chapter 2 of Acts tells us that when "they were all together in one place," Jesus sent the Holy Spirit to them. We call this "Pentecost Day," because that was the name of the Jewish holiday when it happened. Winds blew and something they said looked like fire danced among them. Suddenly all the disciples started speaking in other languages! Crowds gathered. What in the world was going on? Some of the people thought the disciples were drunk. Peter knew one thing — these people in the crowd needed an explanation!

**Sermon Outline**

1. The miracles of Pentecost boggle our minds.

   But there is something more ordinary happening we need to see.

   How could Peter stand up and talk?

2. Something remarkable is happening in the "Trinity of Relationships" for Peter.

   Three relationships — with God, with people in church, and with people outside

   In Peter's relationship with God, he is experiencing forgiveness

   In Peter's relationship with people outside the church, he gets compassion

   In Peter's relationship with fellow disciples, they stand in humility together

3. How are our relationships with each other?

   What do the unchurched outside our doors see in the way we treat each other?

   Trinity of Relationships exercise to focus people on an area in need of healing

4. Conflict in the church can prevent new people from joining.

   One church's story (a story of subtle conflict seen by visitors that stops church's growth)

   When we are right with each other, we make room for others and for God

   It is right all of a sudden

**Benediction**: May God guide our wills to obey; may God guide our hearts to forgive; may God guide our spirits to be set free, in Jesus' name. Amen.

---

---

**Sermon Title:** *Catalytic Conversations*

**Scripture:** Isaiah 43:15–19; John 4:7–10, 16–29

**Theme:** Just talking with someone can change a life.

**Symbol:** Put a "well" up by your prayer wall, using a garden fountain. Prepare a bulletin insert: an invitation tailored to your church.

**Call to Worship**

> *Leader:* Lift up your lives!
> *People:* **Every moment, day and night, is filled with the presence of God.**
> *Leader:* God in Christ has touched earthly life with heavenly possibilities.
> *People:* **May the Spirit teach us anew to see God among us.**
> *All:* **May our lives shimmer with holy moments all around!**

**Show and Tell:** Look for someone who came to church for the first time as an adult. Don't overlook your elderly people. I was surprised to learn that our 85-year-old saint of the church became a Christian at age 25 after a friend invited him to church! You want someone with a clear memory of what life was like *before* having the experience of God's love. Coach him or her to especially tell about any particular person who ushered him or her into the church, and why that helped. This week, unlike last week, the "Show and Tell" is not incorporated into the body of the sermon. Decide whether it will be most effective placed before or after the sermon. Pray for this changed life as he or she shares!

**Scripture Sentences:** John is one of four books of the New Testament that tell the story of Jesus' life. Each of the gospels — Matthew, Mark, Luke, and John — has its own way of portraying Jesus. John's gospel is the only one that includes the story we're going to work with today. Jesus talks with a woman at a village well. This is the longest conversation Jesus has in any of the gospels. It is a very unusual story. In Jesus' culture, public conversations between unrelated men and women were taboo. Also, Jesus and the woman were from different religious and ethnic groups. He was a Jew. She was a Samaritan. The conversation should never have happened according to the rules of the day. But it did.

**Sermon Outline**

1. Tell me one life that has changed this week because of our ministry.

   The priority of a growing church in California (TransformedLives. com)

   Jesus certainly changed the life of the woman at the well

2. What did Jesus do for her?

   He reached out across cultural barriers to have a conversation

   Kamal's story (or other story about conversation making a difference in a life)

3. God's power can make genuine conversation into a life-changing experience.

   Statistics on why people come to church and stay

   You are the reason people come and stay

4. Will you start a conversation that could change someone's life?

   Marta's story (or story about someone invited to your church who was changed)

   Invitation in bulletin for you to invite someone

**Benediction:** May God guide our eyes to see; may God guide our ears to listen; may God guide our conversations to make a difference, in Jesus' name. Amen.

## WEEK 5 OF THE E-VENT

**Sermon Title**: *Healing Hospitality*

**Scripture**: Genesis 18:1−5; Mark 2:1−12

**Theme**: The church is the house of the Lord. So how are we doing?

**Symbol**: Ask your greeters at each door to offer an extra-special welcome to people as they enter the church. Give each person a seasonally appropriate, hospitable gesture. How about lemonade in the summer, hot chocolate in winter, a towel if it's raining!

### Call to Worship

> *Leader*: Lift up our church!
> *People*: **The body of Christ, gathered in this place,**
>      **welcomes the Spirit among us.**
> *Leader*: We pray for every heart and every hearth to be
>      touched by Jesus today.
> *People*: **May there be no stranger or alien, only new**
>      **friends in Christ.**
> *All*: **We are all members of God's household!**

**Show and Tell**: Ask a very new member of your church to share what her or his first experience of the church was like. Encourage the member to share honestly what worked and didn't work to create the feeling of being welcome. You don't want to pressure this person, (see chapter 5 about "using" new members!), but if the person is outgoing, this would be great. Your goal is to have someone who has been there less than two years talk about her or his first experiences at the church. Because this person is still around, surely there was more positive than negative in the experience, or the person wouldn't have stayed! But encourage honesty and thank her or him before the congregation for courage and candor.

**Scripture Sentences:** Mark is probably the very first gospel that was written. Out of the four gospels (Matthew, Mark, Luke, and John), Mark is the shortest. All of the gospels tell the story of Jesus' life, each in its own way. Mark's story about the paralyzed man going through the roof is also in Matthew and Luke, but Mark is the only one that tells the story as though Jesus is in someone's home — possibly his own!

**Sermon Outline**

1. Jesus is at his house.

> Have you ever thought about Jesus having a home?
>
> Internal and external barriers can keep us from bringing people to Jesus

2. Internal barriers exist inside our heads.

> Mark's story (or another story about friends reluctant to share their faith)
>
> Even pastors deal with fear about sharing their faith
>
> Think of evangelism as sharing something you enjoy with someone you like

3. External barriers also must be overcome.

> Neighborhood association meeting story (or your own tale of being excluded)
>
> Does our church have any barriers that keep people from getting to Jesus?
>
> Take a virtual tour

4. We welcome guests into Jesus' house, the church.

> Use the mats in the bulletin for people to identify potential barriers
>
> Elizabeth's story (or a story that shows someone meeting Jesus at the church)
>
> Bring the mats forward

5. Let's pray that every guest meets Jesus here, from the front porch on.

**Benediction**: May God guide our doors to open; may God guide our hearts to welcome; may God guide our hands to receive, in Jesus' name. Amen.

---

---

**Sermon Title**: *Faith Focus*

**Scripture**: Proverbs 3:1–8; Matthew 14:22–33

**Theme**: Jesus is always with us. But that means we may wind up in places we wouldn't have gone on our own!

**Symbol**: Park a boat in the narthex! If you have an artist in your church, you can also have him or her paint, or draw, or develop, a picture of Jesus getting in the boat with the disciples, as described at the end of the sermon. Set up the easel so that the painting can be done throughout the service. (Your artist can have some of it done ahead of time so that it is mostly finished by service's end). Carry out the painting at the end of the service and place it beside the narthex boat.

**Call to Worship**

> *Leader*: Lift up our future!
> *People*: **We lift our coming days to the Lord!**
> *Leader*: We trust the tomorrow God will give us.
> *People*: **God plans to do far more with us than we could ask or imagine!**
> *All*: **Resurrection is the future for all who follow Jesus Christ.**

**Show and Tell**: Has the E-vent changed someone's life? Ask them to tell about it. Perhaps someone has made a commitment to Christ. Who learned something tremendously important and has a commitment to follow through with new habits? You might ask two or three people to share their experiences in a "popcorn" style. Help them hone what they want to say to three to four sentences. If they can be heard, have them stand from where they are in the congregation to speak. If not, ask them to slip quietly to a mike during the sermon, all together, and be ready to share quickly, one right after the other.

**Scripture Sentences**: The New Testament is the part of the Bible that was written in Greek, rather than in Hebrew. Some people call the New Testament the "Greek Scriptures." It contains the four gospels, the history book "Acts," and many amazing letters to churches from leaders of the early church. The first book in the New Testament is a gospel, a story of Jesus' life, and it's written by Matthew. Matthew tells a remarkable story of Jesus walking on water. This is after ***another*** story about Jesus feeding a crowd of more than 5,000 people. You will understand the walking-on-water story better if you know that when the Bible talks about the sea, it is not just talking about a physical body of water. The sea is a symbol for chaos in the Bible. When Jesus walks across the water, he is also walking above the chaos of this world. He is completely in charge.

**Sermon Outline**

1. Have you ever seen someone you know well but didn't recognize?

   Walter and Jean's story (or your own tale about not recognizing someone)

   The disciples don't recognize Jesus either

2. There are times it seems that Jesus is far away.

   Every congregation has storms

   We are never alone

3. Jesus didn't intend for Peter to walk on the water.

   Jesus wanted the disciples to be expecting him

   Are we expecting Jesus at our church?

4. Jesus is always with us.

   We must be alert to Christ's presence

   Show and tell "popcorn-style" to highlight how Christ has been present

5. One small change, consistently implemented, can change our ability to see Jesus.

   Small church's story (or story of a church making a small change to big effect)

   Seeing Jesus is no happenstance. It's a cultivated habit

6. My commitment is for 10 minutes of prayer during every meeting.

   Now comes the slow, steady work of letting the Spirit make changes in us.

   Do you think Jesus can come across time to our boat here?

7. Jesus gets back into the boat with Peter.

   Imagine the picture of Jesus climbing into the boat to be with us

   Where will he lead us next?

**Benediction**: May God guide our hearts to trust; may God guide our fears to cease; may God guide our future to glorify Jesus Christ! Amen.

# CHAPTER 9

# Prayers for Worship

Churches pray in very different ways. We live in a quick, highly verbal culture, where most of us don't have much silence. We go through the days with the radio on in the car, the TV on at home, air conditioner whirring, people talking. It doesn't change much when we get to church. There's a lot of talk and buzz. That can be great. It's community.

However, God is in the silence as well as in the noise. The church has always known that we must "brave the silence" if we want to go much further in our relationships with God than the handshake phase! Unless you're Quaker or a monastic, it's likely that your church talks a great deal, and that there's little silence.

Your people are being very brave during the E-vent. They're praying right out loud and talking with each other about their faith. And they're taking another edge-of-the-cliff risk. They're praying alone. Deeply. Every day. Will you give them a chance to take that one rung deeper? Will you structure worship so that they have true silence together?…no music in the background,…no long pastoral prayer. Risk a time together, in silence, with God.

Minutes of silence in worship can seem very foreign. When I was a pastor, I took my first long, individual prayer retreat, with 10 days of silence, in a monastery. Talk about macho! Going on that retreat was not half as terrifying as asking my congregation to pray in silence for three minutes. I looked at my watch after three minutes. Oh, wow! It had only been 37 seconds. I tapped my watch. The second hand tortoised around. My hands started to sweat, not glow. Our energetic "missions and outreach" lady shifted in her seat. (This was the forceful, extroverted one who wasn't all that thrilled with *everything* I had instigated.) She shifted in her seat again.

I felt as if I were timing a contraction.

Six months later, we changed the worship service one Sunday and didn't do the silence. My missions and outreach lady asked why we'd changed the way we always do the prayer. She said the whole service felt "off."

Will you try? The E-vent will give you an excuse. Everyone is expecting a different type of prayer together. (Look at every Sunday's prayer in the prayer exercises in *Unbinding Your Heart*.) Trust me, the time will be longest for the person leading the prayer! Use your watch. Here are instructions. Your people are ready. They have been praying this week. We need to be able to pray for real.

### Intercession as a Whole Church, Together

#### *First, Describe the Prayer*

The pastor, or prayer leader, could explain the prayer this way, "We now have time to pray together as a church. We are going to pray for four things. We'll pray for

- each other,
- for each of our families,
- for the church and
- that the people with whom we each come into contact this week see God.

"We'll pray for three minutes, mostly in silence. To get ready, sit comfortably, with your backs straight and your feet on the floor. I will open and close the prayer. Let's all concentrate on the same thing, pray for the same thing, but let's do it in silence. I'll just say a phrase like 'we pray for each other.' Then we can all pray silently for the people in this room. After about a minute, I'll say another phrase, like '...for our families,' or '...for the people we'll each come into contact with this week,' and we'll each pray for that group of people, okay? You might want to hold your hands, palms together, little fingers touching, in your lap. Think of holding the people 'shrunk down' into your hands. Your hands can become Christ's hands. Let's just see what God does with this, all right? Get comfortable and let's start."

When people are settled to pray, start. Keep your prayer very short. Direct people to God and keep the prayer focused. The first week you may want to keep the total prayer to about three minutes. By Week 6 of the E-vent, you should be able to pray in silence together for four minutes, with the only sound being your opening and closing, and the spoken cues to change the people you're praying for.

### Now Pray the Prayer

Here are the actual words I would speak to direct the congregation into silent prayer:

"Holy God, we've prayed as individuals this week. We've prayed together in our small groups. Please use us now as a whole church, to pray together. Let us feel your presence." (Pause for 10 seconds.)

"We pray for each other — for every person in this room." (40–60 seconds of silence)

"We pray for each of our families." (40–60 seconds of silence)

"We pray for the church." (40–60 seconds of silence)

"We pray for the people each one of us will come into contact with this week." (40–60 seconds of silence)

"In Jesus' name we pray. Amen."

Please try this silent prayer together. Our people need to learn silent prayers that we can all do. Sound and speaking flood our days, parch our spiritual lives. The E-vent is a time to experiment with impunity! Silence scares us. Being together removes some of the threat and provides moral support (i.e., "Well, if **Lester** can do this, so can I!").

Help your people experience the wellsprings of the Spirit. Help them experience silence together. After a while, resonance permeates the silence. God will meet us there. Many people experience silence that is not lonely for the first time in their lives when they pray with others from their church. Please give your people the chance.

# CHAPTER 10

# A Gift for You Musicians!

Four fabulous musicians have agreed to help you with your E-vent. Each of them serves a very different congregation. Each works with quite different styles of music. They have read *Unbinding Your Heart.* They have worked with these sermons and each has sculpted suggestions for how they will set your service alive with music!

Sources for the hymns and music these musicians have selected are located in footnotes at the end of this chapter. Download additional resources and suggestions from *www.Gracenet.info.* (See page 82 for your password.)

Now, let them give us their best suggestions for each week of the E-vent! These plans are what they would do in their own churches. Nothing is watered down. Nothing is dumbed down. These aren't generic, least-common-denominator, homogenized worship! Here are four originals, giving us their best shots. Musicians! Worshipers! Rejoice!

## Raquel Martínez

Dr. Raquel M. Martínez has been described as the "Dean of Hispanic Music," and "one of the most inspirational musicians — and people — I've ever met." She edited (orchestrated) the wonderful United Methodist Hispanic hymnal *Mil Voces Para Celebrar.* Raquel is a national authority on Latin, Hispanic and Caribbean music. Her passion for this glorious music sparkles across a dinner table, a phone line and certainly resonates through a sanctuary. We will all be blessed by her participation in this project!

## Joyce Meredith

Dr. Joyce Meredith is the Worship Team Leader (music director) and Leadership Team Chair (a.k.a. Board chair!) for New Life Community United Methodist Church in Hebron, Ohio, a rapidly growing, new church start. Hebron is a small town. The church has a range of socio-economic and educational backgrounds. They intentionally structure music around the play list of the local contemporary Christian radio station to help their people tie in church with their normal days. Drop by one Sunday — you won't believe the spirit of this church! Joyce is a trained pianist and has directed choirs for years. Her day job is as Special Assistant to the President of Denison University.

| Michael Graham | Raymond Wise |
|---|---|

**Michael Graham**

Michael Graham has served Woodmont Christian Church as Music Director/ Organist for 21 years. He also teaches choral music at Nashville School of the Arts. Woodmont is a large, thoughtful, primarily Caucasian church filled with Nashville musicians and stunning music! One Sunday morning, I (MGR) heard the choir sing Thomas Tallis (Henry VIII's court musician), then an acoustic guitar medley of hymns by a guy who played backup for the Beatles. Then Reba McEntire's fiddler, the principal cellist of the Nashville Symphony and an orthopedic surgeon on mandolin accompanied the first through third graders' choir singing spirituals! You musicians know the type of inspiring, gifted and gracious musician it takes to bring together and nurture so many gifted and growing talents.

**Raymond Wise**

The Rev. Raymond Wise is a professor of music at Ohio State University, Denison University and Trinity Lutheran Seminary. He is dedicated to training complete musicians. He is founder and President of Raise Productions, a gospel music production company in Columbus, Ohio. Raise's Choirs have recorded numerous CDs and have toured extensively through the United States and Europe. He serves as Associate Minister and Choir Director at Faith Ministries Interdenominational Church. Raymond is a prolific and distinguished composer.

| Raquel Martínez | Joyce Meredith |
|---|---|

**"Holy/Santo"**
FWS
This song is from the Salvadoran mass. Sing in both languages; choir may want to sing it first to help the congregation learn it.

*Gathering*

**"Talk about It (Say So)"**
*Nicole C. Mullen*

**"Whom Shall I Send?"**
UMH

*Worship*

**"Let Everything That Has Breath"**
*Matt Redman*
A great one to open worship. We like the Jeremy Camp version.

**"Enviado soy de Dios / Sent Out in Jesus' Name"**
GP2 and LLC

**"Called as Partners in Christ's Service"**
CH

**"I Could Sing of Your Love Forever"**
*Martin Smith*
A classic worship song.

**"Cuando el pobre / When the Poor Ones"**
LLC

**"How Can I Keep from Singing"**
*Chris Tomlin*
A new song from Tomlin, a master of praise music.

*Offering*

**"If We Are the Body"**
*Casting Crowns*
A rockin' indictment of "business as usual" in the church.

*General Suggestion*

*Gente Nueva* is a set of two cassettes featuring Hispanic/Latino music (one vocal, one instrumental accompaniment). It can be ordered from Discipleship Resources, P.O. Box 840, Nashville, TN 37202–0840. Phone: 615-340-7068, Fax: 615-340-1789

*Closing*

**"In the Blink of an Eye"**
*Mercy Me*

Sources for the songs in this column are abbreviated as follows: *Mil Voces para Celebrar* (MVPC), Abingdon Press; *The Faith We Sing* (FWS), Abingdon Press; *United Methodist Hymnal* (UMH), Abingdon Press; *Chalice Hymnal* (CH), Chalice Press; *Global Praise* (GP), GBGMusik; *Libro de Liturgia y Canción* (LLC), Augsburg Fortress Press; *New Century Hymnal* (NCH), Pilgrim Press.

| Michael Graham | Raymond Wise |
|---|---|

**Michael Graham**

*Processional*

**"God Is Here!"**
This lovely hymn tells why we are gathered and admonishes us to "keep faithful to the gospel and to work God's purpose out."

*Invitational*

**"Joy to the World"**
The most poignant part of the first sermon is the story about the little girl helping her grandfather read the Christmas story. Why not shake everyone up with a well-known Christmas hymn that will keep the story alive and start wheels a turnin'?

*Communion*

**"These I Lay Down"**
As this service moves to God's table, how appropriate to allow people to "lay down" the things that would hinder them from being used of God.

*Anthem*

**"If Ye Love Me"**
*Thomas Tallis, Oxford*

**Raymond Wise**

Key to themes in this column: (1) Sharing the Gospel, (2) Leading Others to Christ, (3) Testimony, (4) Following the Leading of the Holy Spirit/Obedience, (5) Baptism

**"Lift Him Up"**
*Johnson Oatman, Jr.*
STYLE: Hymn
THEME(S):1, 2

**"I Will Trust In The Lord'**
*Traditional Spiritual*
STYLE: Congregational Spiritual
THEME(S): 4

**"This Little Light of Mine'**
*Traditional Spiritual*
STYLE: Congregational Spiritual
THEME(S): 1

**"He Has Done Great Things For Me"**
*Jessy Dixon*
STYLE: Gospel Song
THEME(S): 1, 3

**"Order My Steps"**
*Glenn Burleigh*
STYLE: Gospel Song
THEME(S): 4

**"He's Counting On You"**
*Raymond Wise*
STYLE: Gospel Song
THEME(S): 1
Raise Publishing Company (RACH410-80)

**"What Shall I Render"**
*Margaret Douroux*
STYLE: Gospel Song
THEME(S): 4

All songs in this column are from *Chalice Hymnal* (Chalice Press) unless otherwise noted.

All songs in this column are from the *African American Heritage Hymnal* unless otherwise noted.

| Raquel Martínez | Joyce Meredith |
|---|---|

**"They'll Know We Are Christians' /
"Somos uno en Espíritu"**
(English in FWS; Spanish in MVPC

**"Cristo, quiero ser Cristiano" /
"Lord, I Want to Be a Christian"**
Spanish in MVPC; English in UMH, CH

**"Jesus Christ Sets Free to Serve"**
GP 2
Sing a capella, accompanied by drum only.

**"Freely, Freely"**
UMH

**"Cuán glorioso es el cambio" /
"Since Jesus Came into My Heart"**
Spanish in MVPC; English in FWS
Encourage the congregation to also sing the
Spanish; it may have to be just the refrain.

*Gathering*
**"Sing a Song"**
  *Third Day*
  One of a multitude of great songs by this
  prolific Christian rock band with the blues
  rock sound.

*Worship*
**"Beautiful One"**
  *Tim Hughes*
  A driving beat, and very singable.

**"My Savior, My God"**
  *Aaron Schust*
  Based on a hymn entitled "I Am Not Skilled
  to Understand."

**"You Are My King"**
  *Newsboys*
  Based on the Charles Wesley hymn
  "Amazing Love."

*Offering*
**"Live Out Loud"**
  *Stephen Curtis Chapman*
  Playful, fun and rockin', this one celebrates
  what it means to live in Christ.

*Closing*
**"How Great Is Our God"**
  *Chris Tomlin*
  Beautiful in its simplicity and eminently
  singable, this one lends itself to wonderful
  three-part harmony.

Sources for the songs in this column are abbreviated
as follows: *Mil Voces para Celebrar* (MVPC), Abingdon
Press; *The Faith We Sing* (FWS), Abingdon Press;
*United Methodist Hymnal* (UMH), Abingdon Press;
*Chalice Hymnal* (CH), Chalice Press; *Global Praise*
(GP), GBGMusik; *Libro de Liturgia y Canción* (LLC),
Augsburg Fortress Press; *New Century Hymnal*
(NCH), Pilgrim Press.

| Michael Graham | Raymond Wise |
|---|---|

**Michael Graham**

*Processional*

**"All People That on Earth Do Dwell"**
A familiar tune (Doxology) and an old text with positive vibes emanating throughout.

*Invitational*

**"Lift Every Voice and Sing"**
This sermon reminds me that we meet people where they are. Music is often a place of spiritual linking.

*Communion*

**"What Is This Place"**

*Anthem suggestion*

**"Serve the Coming Days"**
*Dale Wood, Sacred Music Press*

**Raymond Wise**

Key to themes in this column: (1) What difference does Christ make in your life? (2) God wants all to be saved (3) Jesus is the light who shines in a dark world (4) When life gets dark, God will bring light (5) Be obedient whatever the cost (6) Don't be afraid to witness (7) Joy in serving God

**"Love Lifted Me"**
*James Rowe*
STYLE: Hymn
THEME(S): 1

**"Since Jesus Came into My Heart"**
*Rufus H. Mc Daniel*
STYLE: Hymn
THEME(S): 1

**"I Have Decided to Follow Jesus"**
*Indian Folk Melody*
STYLE: Folk Melody
THEME(S): 5, 7

**"Real, Real, Jesus Is Real To Me"**
*Traditional Spiritual*
STYLE: Congregational Spiritual
THEME(S): 1

**"He Touched Me"**
*William Gaither*
STYLE: Gospel Song
THEME(S): 1

**"I Really Love The Lord"**
*Jimmy Dowell*
STYLE: Gospel Song
THEME(S): 1

**"Yes God Is Real"**
*Kenneth Morris*
STYLE: Gospel Song
THEME(S): 1

All songs in this column are from *Chalice Hymnal* (Chalice Press) unless otherwise noted.

All songs in this column are from the *African American Heritage Hymnal* unless otherwise noted.

| Raquel Martínez | Joyce Meredith |
|---|---|
| **"Lord, Listen to Your Children Praying"**<br>FWS<br>I would close the two minutes of prayer with this song. Either have the choir sing it, or the congregation will need to learn it beforehand.<br><br>**"Take Time to Be Holy"**<br>UMH<br><br>**"Oh deja que el Señor" / "Spirit Song"**<br>Spanish in MVPC; English in UMH and CH<br><br>**"Nurtured by the Spirit"**<br>GP 2<br><br>**"Come and Find the Quiet Center"**<br>FWS | *Gathering*<br>**"Presence (My Heart's Desire)"**<br>*Newsboys*<br><br>*Worship*<br>**"Everlasting God"**<br>*Brenton Brown, Ken Riley*<br>It's hard to find upbeat music for a prayer theme, but this one seems to fit the bill. We like the Lincoln Brewster recording that is getting a lot of airplay right now.<br><br>**"Open the Eyes of My Heart"**<br>*Paul Baloche*<br>This one rocks, too.<br><br>**"Word of God Speak"**<br>*Mercy Me*<br>This one will bring the tempo down for a prayerful atmosphere.<br><br>*Offering*<br>**"Be Still and Know"**<br>*Stephen Curtis Chapman*<br>Beautiful melody, beautiful lyrics. What more can I say?<br><br>*Closing*<br>**"Holiness"**<br>*Scott Underwood*<br>Another simple but beautiful song with opportunities for great harmony. |

Sources for the songs in this column are abbreviated as follows: *Mil Voces para Celebrar* (MVPC), Abingdon Press; *The Faith We Sing* (FWS), Abingdon Press; *United Methodist Hymnal* (UMH), Abingdon Press; *Chalice Hymnal* (CH), Chalice Press; *Global Praise* (GP), GBGMusik; *Libro de Liturgia y Canción* (LLC), Augsburg Fortress Press; *New Century Hymnal* (NCH), Pilgrim Press.

| Michael Graham | Raymond Wise |
|---|---|
| *Processional* | Key to themes in this column: (1) Prayer (2) Wait on God for guidance and direction (3) Hear the voice of God (4) Obedience to God in spite of the situation (5) Seek God first (6) Rest in and depend on God |
| **"All Creatures of Our God and King"** <br> Another motivating, wonderful hymn. | |
| *Invitational* | **"Guide Me Oh Thou Great Jehovah"** <br> *William Williams* <br> STYLE: Hymn <br> THEME(S): 2 |
| **"Lord, You Give the Great Commission"** | |
| *Communion* | **"What a Friend We Have in Jesus"** <br> *Joseph M. Scriven* <br> STYLE: Hymn <br> THEME(S): 1 |
| **"Spirit of God, Descend upon My Heart"** | |
| *Anthem suggestion* | **"Come By Here Lord"** <br> *Traditional Spiritual* <br> STYLE: Spiritual <br> THEME(S): 1, 5 |
| **"Deep Waters"** <br> *Pepper Choplin, Beckenhorst Press* | |
| | **"Jesus on the Mainline"** <br> *Traditional Spiritual* <br> STYLE: Congregational Spiritual <br> THEME(S): 1 |
| | **"Give Me a Clean Heart"** <br> *Margaret Douroux* <br> STYLE: Gospel <br> THEME(S): 1, 4 |
| | **"Lead Me, Guide Me"** <br> *Doris Akers* <br> STYLE: Gospel <br> THEME(S): 2 |
| | **"Precious Lord"** <br> *Thomas Dorsey* <br> STYLE: Gospel <br> THEME(S): 2 |
| | **"Come unto Jesus"** <br> *Raymond Wise* <br> STYLE: Gospel Song <br> THEME(S): 6 <br> Raise Publishing Company (RAGO142-91) |
| All songs in this column are from *Chalice Hymnal* (Chalice Press) unless otherwise noted. | All songs in this column are from the *African American Heritage Hymnal* unless otherwise noted. |

| Raquel Martínez | Joyce Meredith |
|---|---|

**Raquel Martínez**

**"Somos uno en Cristo" /**
**"We Are One in Christ Jesus"**
   Spanish and English in MVPC and FWS

**"Miren qué bueno" / "O Look and Wonder"**
   Spanish and English in FWS; Spanish in MVPC
   This is a good song to use for the passing of the peace.

**"Mirad cuán bueno" /**
**"Behold, How Good and Delightful"**
   English and Spanish in LLC

**"Somos el cuerpo de Cristo" /**
**"We Are the Body of Christ "**
   English and Spanish in *Flor y Canto, segunda edición*, OCP Publications, Portland, Oreg.

**"Un mandamiento nuevo" /**
**"Jesus a New Commandment Has Given"**
   Spanish and English in GP 3 and NCH.

**"Together We Serve"**
   FWS

Sources for the songs in this column are abbreviated as follows: *Mil Voces para Celebrar* (MVPC), Abingdon Press; *The Faith We Sing* (FWS), Abingdon Press; *United Methodist Hymnal* (UMH), Abingdon Press; *Chalice Hymnal* (CH), Chalice Press; *Global Praise* (GP), GBGMusik; *Libro de Liturgia y Canción* (LLC), Augsburg Fortress Press; *New Century Hymnal* (NCH), Pilgrim Press.

**Joyce Meredith**

*Gathering*

**"I Believe"**
   *Third Day*
   A wonderfully rough and bluesy rock song, this is Third Day's take on First Corinthians 13:13.

*Worship*

**"Let It Rise"**
   *Holland Davis*
   This is an old classic of the praise genre.

**"Holy Is the Lord"**
   *Louie Giglio, Chris Tomlin*

**"Made to Worship"**
   *Chris Tomlin, Ed Cash, Stephan Sharp*
   A beautiful, very singable song celebrating Christian community.

*Offering*

**"Take My Life"**
   *Third Day*
   A soft, sweet song of repentance. Third Day does it with only acoustic guitar accompaniment.

*Closing*

**"I Want to Be Clean (Purify Me Jesus)"**
   *Danny Myrick, Tony Wood*
   Another slow one, but with a beat and a nice counterpoint part in the chorus.

| Michael Graham | Raymond Wise |
|---|---|
| *Processional* | Key to themes in this column: (1) Stand up for Jesus (2) Stand together in God's Love (3) Stand for others who need to know God (4) Developing closer and better relationships with God and others (5) Show love toward one another (6) Worthiness to witness after being forgiven |
| **"On Pentecost They Gathered"** *Chalice Hymnal* has a version with a descant that can be sung by sopranos and tenors on verse four. | |
| *Invitational* | **"Leaning on the Everlasting Arms"** *Elisha A. Hoffman* STYLE: Hymn THEME(S): 4 |
| **"Wind upon the Waters"** | |
| *Communion* | **"Stand Up, Stand Up for Jesus"** *George Duffield, Jr.* STYLE: Hymn THEME(S): 4 |
| **"Holy Spirit, Truth Divine"** | |
| *Anthem suggestion* | **"We Are Soldiers"** *Traditional* STYLE: Congregational Spiritual THEME(S): 1, 2 |
| **"New Heart and New Spirit"** *Alice Jordan, Cantate* | |
| | **"We Shall Overcome"** *Traditional* STYLE: Protest Song THEME(S): 2, 3, 5 |
| | **"Somebody Prayed for Me"** *Dorothy Norwood & Alvin Darling* STYLE: Gospel THEME(S): 3, 5 |
| | **"We Offer Christ to You"** *Joel Britton* STYLE: Gospel THEME(S): 1, 2, 3 |
| | **"I'll Stand"** *Raymond Wise* STYLE: Concert Spiritual THEME(S): 1, 2, 3 Raise Publishing Company (RASA203-95) |
| All songs in this column are from *Chalice Hymnal* (Chalice Press) unless otherwise noted. | All songs in this column are from the *African American Heritage Hymnal* unless otherwise noted. |

| Raquel Martínez | Joyce Meredith |
|---|---|
| **"The Servant Song"**<br>FWS | ***Gathering***<br>**"The Change"**<br>*Stephen Curtis Chapman* |
| **"People Need the Lord"**<br>FWS<br>This could be used as a response to the gospel of John's reading; or in some other appropriate part of the service. | ***Worship***<br>**"Trading My Sorrows"**<br>*Darrell Evans*<br>An exuberant and driving rock song! |
| **"Pass It On"**<br>CH | **"Cry Out to Jesus"**<br>*Third Day*<br>One of Third Day's slow songs, we've found this one speaks to people in a profound way. |
| **"Grato es contar la historia"** /<br>**"I Love to Tell the Story"**<br>Spanish in MVPC; English in UMH and CH | **"Only Grace"**<br>*Matthew West* |
| **"You Are the Seed"** / **"Sois la semilla"**<br>English and Spanish in UMH and CH;<br>Spanish in MVPC | ***Offering***<br>**"Mountain of God"**<br>*Third Day* |
| | ***Closing***<br>**"Remember Your Chains"**<br>*Stephen Curtis Chapman*<br>An intensely powerful song! |

Sources for the songs in this column are abbreviated as follows: *Mil Voces para Celebrar* (MVPC), Abingdon Press; *The Faith We Sing* (FWS), Abingdon Press; *United Methodist Hymnal* (UMH), Abingdon Press; *Chalice Hymnal* (CH), Chalice Press; *Global Praise* (GP), GBGMusik; *Libro de Liturgia y Canción* (LLC), Augsburg Fortress Press; *New Century Hymnal* (NCH), Pilgrim Press.

| Michael Graham | Raymond Wise |
|---|---|
| *Processional* | Key to themes in this column: (1) Overcoming fears and obstacles to share the gospel (2) Get close to Jesus to receive forgiveness and healing (3) walking on in spite of trials and obstacles |
| **"All Hail the Power of Jesus' Name!"** A favorite in most churches, the title alone should inspire us. | **"Yield Not to Temptation"** *Horatio R. Palmer* STYLE: Hymn THEME(S): 1 |
| *Invitational* **"Wade in the Water"** This sermon reminds me of the pool at Bethesda. Not much happens until we take action. | **"Come and Go with Me to My Father's House"** *Traditional* STYLE: Congregational Spiritual THEME(S): 1 |
| *Communion* **"Lead Me, Lord"** | **"Come to Jesus"** *Traditional* STYLE: Hymn THEME(S): 1, 2 |
| *Anthem suggestion* **"Lord, Make Me an Instrument of Thy Peace"** *Michael Graham, Concordia Publishing Co.* | **"I'm Determined to Walk with Jesus"** *Traditional Spiritual* STYLE: Traditional Spiritual THEME(S): 1 |
| | **"I'm So Glad Jesus Lifted Me"** *Traditional* STYLE: Congregational Spiritual THEME(S): 1 |
| | **"Walk Together Children"** *Traditional Spiritual* STYLE: Traditional Spiritual THEME(S): 3 |
| | **"Victory Is Mine"** *Dorothy Norwood & Alvin Darling* STYLE: Gospel THEME(S): 1 |
| All songs in this column are from *Chalice Hymnal* (Chalice Press) unless otherwise noted. | All songs in this column are from the *African American Heritage Hymnal* unless otherwise noted. |

| Raquel Martínez | Joyce Meredith |
|---|---|
| **"Open My Eyes That I May See"** / **"Abre mis ojos a la luz"** <br> English in UMH; Spanish in MVPC. | *Gathering* <br> **"In the Blink of an Eye "** <br> *Mercy Me* |
| **"Stand by Me (When the storms of life are raging)"** <br> UMH and CH | *Worship* <br> **"Lord You Are Good"** <br> *Israel Houghton* <br> Really high energy and gets the crowd going! |
| **"Lonely the Boat"** <br> UMH | **"Let Everything That Has Breath"** <br> *Matt Redman* |
| **"Ven, Espíritu de Dios"** / **"Spirit of the Living God"** <br> Spanish in MVPC; English in UMH <br> Can be used as a prayer of consecration | **"Lifesong"** <br> *Mercy Me* <br> This one is singable, lends itself to harmony, and really rocks! |
| **"Lord, You Have Come to the Lakeshore"** / **"Tú has venido a la orilla"** <br> Spanish and English in MVPC, CH and UMH | *Offering* <br> **"Dive"** <br> *Stephen Curtis Chapman* <br> Great rhythms build anticipation for the rousing chorus in this song. You can't sit still with this one. |
| **Lord, You Give the Great Commission** <br> CH and UMH | *Closing* <br> **"He Reigns"** <br> *Newsboys* <br> This incredible song sings the power of God's people united across the whole Earth. |

Sources for the songs in this column are abbreviated as follows: *Mil Voces para Celebrar* (MVPC), Abingdon Press; *The Faith We Sing* (FWS), Abingdon Press; *United Methodist Hymnal* (UMH), Abingdon Press; *Chalice Hymnal* (CH), Chalice Press; *Global Praise* (GP), GBGMusik; *Libro de Liturgia y Canción* (LLC), Augsburg Fortress Press; *New Century Hymnal* (NCH), Pilgrim Press.

# The E-vent in Gear

## *Flowcharts, Calendars, Forms, Organizational Help*

### with Catherine Riddle Caffey

### Chapter 11 Highlights

- The E-vent in Gear!
- Full List of Forms to Download
- Four Specific Forms
  - Unbinding the Gospel Series Flowchart, How the Series Works *(Pastor Form #2)*
  - E-vent Leadership Team Diagram *(Pastor Form #4)*
  - 10-Minute Prayer Exercise for the Beginning of All Team Meetings *(Prayer Form #36)*
  - Pastor's Checklist of E-vent Planning Milestones *(Pastor Form #9c)*

### The E-vent in Gear!

#### *Ready...Set...Organize!*

Chapter 11 is the E-vent in gear! Here are forms, lists and organizational aids to help you prepare for and provide your church with an integrated, organized E-vent. You organizers are great. Our work dovetails when teachers teach and intercessors pray and pastors preach and the brilliant organized ones do their thing! Thank you all. Organizing an E-vent is a great big job. But as Tom Hanks said

We have gifts that differ according to the grace given to us: prophecy, in proportion to faith; ministry, in ministering; the teacher, in teaching; the exhorter, in exhortation; the giver, in generosity; the leader, in diligence; the compassionate, in cheerfulness.
*Romans 12:6–8*

**123**

about playing baseball, "If it weren't hard, it wouldn't be great."[1] And you all are doing great!

Catherine Caffey has helped put the organizational wheels under the E-vent. Catherine lives in Nashville. She served as Director of Marketing for a billion dollar financial services company in Atlanta for over a decade. Catherine's eyes glisten with delight over flowcharts, color-coding, bullet points and master rosters. Plus, she prays deeply and seriously. She is committed to "Moms in Touch International," praying over children and their schools. She loves the church.

Catherine has created charts, lists, rosters, flowcharts and diagrams for you. We decided to put them on the Web so that we could make them larger, and so that Catherine could indulge her passion for color-coding! We will all delight in her creations. Go to *www.GraceNet.info* to download the forms in all their 8.5" x 11" splendor. ***Your password: Unbinding***.

Here are three forms that you will need right away. Go online for the rest! You administrator/organizers out there: have fun!

[1] *A League of Their Own,* Columbia Pictures Corporation, 1992.

## E-vent Leadership Team Diagram

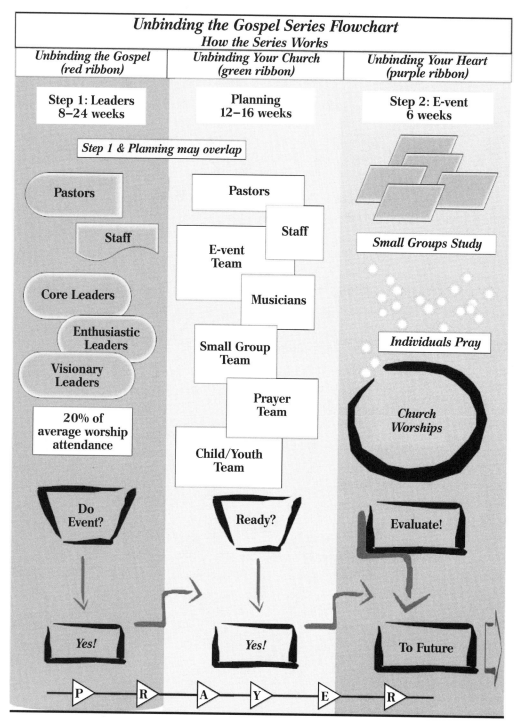

### Unbinding the Gospel Series Flowchart
#### How the Series Works

| Unbinding the Gospel (red ribbon) | Unbinding Your Church (green ribbon) | Unbinding Your Heart (purple ribbon) |
|---|---|---|

**Step 1: Leaders**
**8–24 weeks**

**Planning**
**12–16 weeks**

**Step 2: E-vent**
**6 weeks**

*Step 1 & Planning may overlap*

Pastors

Staff

Core Leaders

Enthusiastic Leaders

Visionary Leaders

20% of average worship attendance

Pastors

Staff

E-vent Team

Musicians

Small Group Team

Prayer Team

Child/Youth Team

*Small Groups Study*

*Individuals Pray*

*Church Worships*

Do Event?

Ready?

Evaluate!

*Yes!*

*Yes!*

To Future

P  R  A  Y  E  R

Pastor Form #2 from www.GraceNet.info, © 2007 by GraceNet, Inc.

*Next Step
Keep going & grow!
Unbinding Your Soul provides the
small group structure for churches
that now WANT to reach out.*

# Unbinding Your Soul

## Introduction

### How to Use This Book

I've spent the last 15 years leading national research projects focused on faith, spirituality and the transformation of Christian communities. I've interviewed or spoken in depth with about two thousand people during this time. Some of them have no connection with organized religion. Many more are Christians—pastors, church leaders, and new and old Christians across the country.[1]

I hear one message clearly: *Most people want real friends.* Most people want to be able to talk honestly about their lives and about significant life issues. Most people have some kind of a spiritual life. Millions of people in and out of churches would love to try an authentic test of a faith community—a confidential, loving, hopeful, real group of people. They'd like to explore, to think about, to talk with other people about God, about Jesus, about what's possible in a human life. Loads of people would like to work with some ancient prayer practices. Christian prayer and community are extraordinary and can be life changing.

I hear something else: *No one wants to be trapped.* We wouldn't buy a car sight unseen. We'd test-drive it. Loads of people who don't go to church would love to try a short, non-obligating, "test-drive" of Christianity—as long as they didn't get stuck. They'd like something short term, intense, and not watered down. A lot of Christians feel the same way. They'd like to try something more "real," more substantial

*Unbinding Your Soul*
**works for:**

- ■ **Small groups that have just finished the E-vent**
- ■ **New churches**
- ■ **New members' classes**
- ■ **Vibrant, growing churches**
- ■ **On-fire groups in typical churches**

**137**

than just dropping by church most Sundays—as long as it wasn't weird, or they didn't commit themselves for too long. So loads of people would like to try the same thing—an experiment in a more substantial type of faith and spirituality, and talking about what's really going on in their lives.

*The predicament:* Hideous cartoons of evangelism lurk in our heads. I've led the only major, national study of evangelism in the seven specific denominations called "Mainline Churches." I can tell you for a fact, after four years of intensive research, that people who don't go to church cringe at the idea of strangers harassing them with humiliating, condescending questions about whether they're saved. But that's **nothing** compared to the horror with which members of churches hear the word "evangelism." The word hits the eardrum. Christians break out in a cold sweat and start lacing on their Adidas$^{TM}$

The purpose of this group is to create a fun, safe place for everyone to have significant conversations.

*Recap:* Most people want to have friends they can trust. They want to talk about significant life and faith issues and to try some classic Christian prayer disciplines. But **no one** wants to sound like a honey-crusted nut bar.[2] No one wants to be stuck in a room with a bunch of loonies. No one wants to embarrass a friend.

*A Solution: Unbinding Your Soul* can provide the foundation for a four-week "test-drive" of Christian friendship, discussion, community, and classic prayer disciplines. I'm going to call it "Your Experiment in Prayer & Community." Use it as a test. See if you like it. Give it your best efforts for four weeks. At the end of the four weeks, you're done. No one will bug you. No one will expect you to stay. After four meetings and three weeks of working with different types of prayer, you'll have a good idea whether this is any kind of fit for you. *The Experiment is Part One of this book.*

*Church People*—I know this is hard. People have told you not to be pushy or rude your whole Christian life. (Or they may **have** told you to be pushy and rude, but you've cowered in corners or wanted to come out swinging.) One way or the other, Christians all over the country are walking around, quietly traumatized by horrific visions of arguing people into bumper sticker truth and forcing pamphlets into the hands of frantically reluctant strangers. Unfortunately, those bad cartoons have stopped many of us from mentioning to our best friends that we love the church we're part of, and that our faith is the core of our lives. I think that's problematic. We don't have to be *quite* such timid woodland creatures. So here's the deal:

1. You don't have to do anything embarrassing.

2. Invite *one* person you really like to be part of the Experiment. Who's a real friend? Who has an interesting life and fascinating ideas on other subjects? With whom do you want to spend some significant time? With whom would *you* like to talk about faith issues and about *your* life? *That's* the person you invite into the Experiment. You can invite your whole golf foursome or your string quartet if you want.

3. I'm giving you all an extra, four-week, pre-Experiment, Warm-Up to help you garner the courage to ask your best friends if they'd like to try the Experiment with you.

***Church groups: Start at Part TWO of this book for your Warm-Up.***

*A Level Playing Field:* Friends of these Christians—thank you for considering being part of The Experiment. You may have had some horrible experience of someone haranguing you with biblical proof-texts or humiliating questions. This group isn't about that. You're not the guinea pig. It's YOUR experiment!

The purpose of this group is to create a fun, safe place for everyone to have significant conversations. The purpose of the group is to think a bit about some big questions—Is there a God? How can I know? How do you pray? What's true about the world? How can we live together best? How should I spend my life? How can I walk with God, every day, learning and not clotting? The purpose of the group is to talk about what *you* want to talk about! What's happening in your life? It will be a new experience for everyone—people who go to church each week, people who don't. This is a level playing field.

No one is selling anything. No one will try to convert or manipulate you.

However, I can't imagine a group of eight or ten people not changing a little if they talk honestly for four meetings, and pray in between. Let me be as honest as I can be about my presuppositions and worldview: I'm a Christian, I believe that God exists, loves us, and wants us to become much more spiritually aware, more hopeful, more deeply connected with other people, more joy-filled, more committed to living a life that's rich with serving other people. (I also believe all that's possible!)

My hope for the outcome of this month together is that you'll get to know each other better and that you will take whatever "next steps"

> The purpose of the group is to think a bit about some big questions—Is there a God? How can I know? How do you pray?

God would like you to take. God can, and will, do amazing things *in our lives* and ***through us*** if we'll just pay attention and follow.

This is a pretty humble process. It isn't rocket science. It's spiritual growth. We trust that God will bless our lives and take us to the next deeper level if we'll talk honestly with each other, listen carefully and respectfully to each other, study bits of the Bible and pray. Four weeks isn't very long, so let's not tiptoe around the main point or fuss around with leading up to it gently. You all are interested enough to agree to meet four times and to pray for three weeks. Let's get started!

Most people want to have friends they can trust. They want to talk about significant life and faith issues and to try some classic Christian prayer disciplines. But *no one* wants to sound like a honey-crusted nut bar. No one wants to be stuck in a room with a bunch of loonies. No one wants to embarrass a friend.

---

[1]The Mainline Evangelism Project was a major, four-year study of highly effective evangelism in seven denominations, made possible by a grant from the Lilly Endowment (Martha Grace Reese, Project Director). Congregations studied were affiliated with the American Baptist Churches, USA, Christian Church (Disciples of Christ), Evangelical Lutheran Church in America, Presbyterian Church USA, Reformed Church in America, United Church of Christ and The United Methodist Church. See *Unbinding the Gospel,* 2nd ed. by Martha Grace Reese (Chalice Press, 2008), the cornerstone book of the *Unbinding the Gospel Series.* The first two pages of this book describe the Series. More information is available at the very end of this book, at *Next Steps.* Look at *www.GraceNet.info* for general information on the Lilly Endowment-funded grants, the purposes of the studies and the current *Unbinding the Gospel Project* grant. A full Wenger-Reese sociological report detailing the statistical results of the *Mainline Evangelism Project* is available at www.GraceNet.info / Download Resources.

[2]Aaron Sorkin, *Studio 60 on the Sunset Strip,* 2007.